Between Faith and Doubt

D1290846

Between Faith and Doubt

Dialogues on Religion and Reason

John Hick

First published 2010 by
PALGRAVE MACMILLAN

Palgrave Macmillan in the UK is an imprint of Macmillan Publishers Limited, registered in England, company number 785998, of Houndmills, Basingstoke, Hampshire RG21 6XS.

Palgrave Macmillan in the US is a division of St Martin's Press LLC, 175 Fifth Avenue, New York, NY 10010.

Palgrave Macmillan is the global academic imprint of the above companies and has companies and representatives throughout the world.

Palgrave® and Macmillan® are registered trademarks in the United States, the United Kingdom, Europe and other countries.

ISBN 978–0–230–25166–3   hardback
ISBN 978–0–230–25167–0   paperback

This book is printed on paper suitable for recycling and made from fully managed and sustained forest sources. Logging, pulping and manufacturing processes are expected to conform to the environmental regulations of the country of origin.

A catalogue record for this book is available from the British Library.

Library of Congress Cataloging-in-Publication Data
Hick, John, 1922–
  Between faith and doubt : dialogues on religion and reason / John Hick.
      p. cm.
  Includes bibliographical references and index.
  ISBN 978–0–230–25166–3 — ISBN 978–0–230–25167–0 (pbk.)
  1. Belief and doubt.   2. Skepticism.   3. Faith.   4. God.
  5. Religion.   I. Title.
  BD215.H53 2010
  210—dc22   2010002693

10   9   8   7   6   5   4   3   2   1
19   18   17   16   15   14   13   12   11   10

Printed and bound in Great Britain by
CPI Antony Rowe, Chippenham and Eastbourne

This book is dedicated to
my youngest grandchild
PHOEBE

Contents

Preface

This short book is meant for you if you are highly sceptical about religion, but not ready to dismiss it entirely, or if you are somewhere on the spectrum between faith and doubt. It consists in a series of dialogues between an imaginary person, David, who views with strong scepticism all beliefs about a transcendent reality, and someone else, John – me – who does believe, on the basis of religious experience, that there is a higher reality beyond the physical and the human.

The dialogues deal with the big questions facing us all. Is there any good reason to believe in God? Or is God a delusion? And what exactly do we mean by God? If not the traditional God of the churches, is there 'something there' in addition to the material universe of which we are part? Are the occasional unusual or 'peak' moments which many people have experienced momentary glimpses of a larger spiritual environment? Is it rational to trust such experiences? If so, what does this show us about the meaning of life? And about what happens after death? In each case both sides of the argument are presented by David and John.

In the dialogues I have sometimes referred to my own experiences during quite a long life – not only moments of compelling religious experience but also the experience of encountering other religions, of being in an earthquake, of being the subject of a heresy trial, of witnessing materialization mediumship.

Some readers may be tempted to skip Dialogues 8 and 9 on neuroscience, thinking that they may be too technical. But I hope that they will resist the temptation and at least look at these pages, for the technical terms are translated into plain English and the information there is in fact rather interesting, and the issues very important.

John Hick

1
Defining the Issue: Naturalism vs. Religion

DAVID: It's good to see you again after all these years, John, and to have a chance to argue again as we used to in university days. I suppose you're still stuck in your web of religious illusion?

JOHN: Good to see you too. And I gather that you're still stuck in your uncritical naturalistic assumption.

DAVID: Except that it's not uncritical. It's the natural 'default' position of the modern mind. I believe that nothing but the natural, or physical, universe exists. There's no supernatural realm beyond it of gods or immortal souls or angels and devils or heaven and hell. There is only this material universe which the sciences are progressively exploring and seeking to understand.

JOHN: That's the naturalistic view. I agree that it's a possibility. But only a possibility. I think that the universe is ambiguous. That is, there can in principle be both complete and consistent naturalistic accounts of it and complete and consistent religious accounts of it, each including an account of the other. The naturalistic account includes religion as a delusion, while the religious account includes the sciences as describing the physical universe, but unable to go beyond that. I'm differing here of course from many religious as well as anti-religious thinkers. But I think you may agree with me about this?

DAVID: I can agree that the universe is ambiguous, but only in the sense that different people can and do understand it in different ways. But it's not inherently ambiguous. It consists simply of matter. It's unimaginably large, and within it very complex chemical structures have developed over thousands of millions of years, including eventually we large-brained human animals who have evolved on this planet, and quite possibly on other planets of other suns in this and other galaxies as well. All this is absolutely fascinating to contemplate, and it's truly awesome to think that we may quite possibly be the only minute bits of the universe that are temporarily conscious of the rest of it. But there's nothing here to suggest a supernatural reality over and above the material universe – except our natural horror at the thought of being the brief products of a vast mindless process which is soon going to extinguish us, going on endlessly as though we had never existed. Religion is very largely an antidote to a natural but generally suppressed fear of this, in other words, fear of death. So I still maintain that naturalism, as you philosophers call it, is not a mere ungrounded assumption but is what our best science has concluded.

JOHN: And I, in contrast, am trying to show you the ambiguity of the universe, over against dogmatic materialism. This is, incidentally, a reversal of roles, because a couple of hundred years ago it was the naturalistic thinker who had to show the dogmatic religious believer that the universe is ambiguous and does not *have* to be understood religiously, while today it's the other way round. It's now we religious people who have to show the materialists that the universe does not *have* to be understood as solely physical and nothing more. Materialism, or in philosophical language physicalism, is not anything scientifically established. It's a jump from the ever advancing success of the sciences in exploring the physical universe to the assumption that there is no other reality than the physical. But it's still only an assumption, though a deeply entrenched one. Indeed, as Thomas Kuhn showed in his *The Structure of Scientific Revolutions*,[1] such assumptions can be so engrained in a generation or a span of generations of scientists (and the wider public whom they influence) that they can be as difficult to argue with or to supersede as the faith of a religious believer. So taking yourself as typical, when for example someone says that sometimes in prayer they are conscious of God as a surrounding invisible personal presence, you will automatically dismiss this as delusion because you think you know that there is no supranatural – which I prefer to 'supernatural' – reality. Right? Or when in some form of religious meditation someone reports experiencing an aspect of their nature that is continuous with a more ultimate transcendent reality, you will likewise automatically regard this as a delusion. And when William James wrote that 'our normal waking consciousness ... is but one special type of consciousness, while all about it, parted from it by the filmiest of screens, there lie potential forms of consciousness entirely different',[2] you automatically dismiss all such ideas? Isn't that so?

DAVID: Yes of course, but this is simply the scientific understanding of the world which has been progressively established during the last three or four centuries and is now – at least in the West – the almost universally accepted world-view, so that if anyone rejects it, it's up to them to give reasons. So I am a Humanist. I believe that there is only this world and this life and nothing beyond – so let's enjoy this life as best we can.

JOHN: Yes, and to clarify, you're not only a humanist in the sense of affirming the dignity and worth of all people, as rational beings, and wanting us all to lead good and happy lives in this world. In that sense we're all humanists; we all want people to lead good and happy lives. But your humanism is what's been both attacked and defended as materialism. And my point is that this is a faith in the sense that it's something intensely believed that nevertheless cannot be proved.

DAVID: Perhaps not proved in the strict logical sense, but it can be shown to be overwhelmingly probable – in contrast to a religious understanding of the world.

JOHN: So you say, but I want to test that claim.

DAVID: Okay. But before we launch out on that let's get rid of a possible misunderstanding. I'm a materialist – or physicalist – in the sense that I believe that nothing but matter exists. But that doesn't mean that we Humanists are materialistic in the sense of being concerned only with material possessions and having no higher interests or ideals. You'll agree, I hope, that physicalism doesn't involve materialism in that sense?

JOHN: No, agreed, of course it doesn't. And while we're getting our language straight, can we, as I've already suggested, keep away from 'supernatural' with its association with the occult, the spooky, ghosts, witches, magic, spells and so on. Let's agree to use instead the less-polluted word 'supranatural' and, for the sake of variety, 'suprasensory'.

DAVID: Yes, by all means. And going back a step, my materialism or physicalism is indeed an assumption in the sense that it's now so well established that we don't have continually to rehearse the reasons for it. In the same way we all operate all the time on the assumption that the 'laws' of nature will continue to hold, and indeed on all sorts of lesser assumptions of daily life, such as that people will normally obey some basic social rules, like driving on their own side of the road. So that naturalism is for me a firm assumption is not in any way a point against it. You would have to undermine the reasons for it if you want me to question it.

JOHN: Yes, I know. And I also hold with the great Scottish philosopher David Hume that the regularities of nature cannot be proved but are nevertheless justifiably assumed. We couldn't live without them. And likewise with such social assumptions as that other drivers will stay on their own side of the road. But your naturalistic assumption is not in the same category. It's not a necessary assumption of daily life but a comprehensive theory which we can accept or reject. You say that the reasons for it are so obvious

that there's no need to rehearse them. But when anyone does rehearse them it turns out that logic doesn't
take them as far as their naturalistic conclusion –
they've only got there by a leap of faith. So let's look
at your supporting reasons for it.

DAVID: Well, take the examples you just offered. Religious people may indeed have the subjective experiences in prayer and meditation that they describe.
I don't need to deny that. But I say that it's a product
of their own minds. Thomas Hobbes put it well: for
someone 'to say that God hath spoken to him in a
dream, is no more than to say he dreamed that God
spake to him'.[3] The purely natural explanation of religious experience is sufficient by itself so that there's
no need to postulate additional unobservable entities.
I appeal here to Ockham's razor: don't multiply entities beyond necessity.

JOHN: I can't help being reminded here of something I read yesterday in Rumi – the great Persian Sufi
mystic:[4]

Think how it is to have a conversation with an embryo.
You might say, 'The world outside is vast and intricate.
There are wheat fields and mountain passes,
And orchards in bloom.
At night there are millions of galaxies, and in sunlight
The beauty of friends dancing at a wedding.'
You ask the embryo why he, or she, stays cooped up
In the dark with eyes closed.
     Listen to the answer.
There is no 'other world'.
I only know what I've experienced
You must be hallucinating.

DAVID: That's nice. But it doesn't prove anything. I still say that mystical experience is purely subjective.

JOHN: Okay. But a caution about that word 'subjective', which can easily lead the unwary astray. All conscious experience is subjective – that is, it occurs in our consciousness and is only accessible to the experiencer. So there's nothing significant about an experience being subjective – it couldn't be otherwise. But you say there is a purely natural explanation for religious experience. What's that?

DAVID: It's part of the natural explanation of religion as a whole. As you know, there are several possibilities. From the point of view of sociology – and if you want to single out one major figure here I suppose it would be Emile Durkheim – religion came about to build and preserve social cohesion. In his study of Australian aborigines he developed the theory that the gods of primal societies were symbols of society itself, for 'a society has all that is necessary to arouse the sensation of the divine in minds, merely by the power it has over them';[5] and he generalized this to cover religion in all its forms. Or, for Karl Marx, religion is 'the opium of the people',[6] giving them comfort in a heartless world, and used as a means of social control by capitalists over their workers. Or, from the psychoanalytic point of view, Sigmund Freud, who was of course the big figure here, said that 'The derivation of religious needs from the infant's helplessness and the longing for the father aroused by it seems to me incontrovertible.'[7] And of course there have been detailed developments and elaborations of each of these since those founding figures. But you know them yourself, and I don't need to spell them out. Don't you see any truth in any of them?

JOHN: Oh yes, I think there's an element of truth in each of them, but I don't think that any of them, or all of them together, constitute the whole truth. It's true that historically religion is largely a social phenomenon. But it's also true that the originating moments of the great world faiths have usually come through remarkable individuals – Zoroaster, the Buddha, Mahavira, Moses, Jesus, Muhammad, Nanak. And it's true that organized religion has typically operated as an instrument of social control. But it's also true that religion has often been the impetus for social change – for example, the Buddhist rejection of the caste structure of Indian society, or the religious motivation of the anti-slavery movement in the West, or the influence of liberation theology in South America, or Christian opposition to apartheid in South Africa. Again, it's true that in difficult or threatening circumstances people may readily take comfort from the thought of a loving heavenly Father who can protect them. And it's also true that many Christians derive comfort from belief in that same God suffering with or for them on the cross. But there are also religions, Buddhism in particular but also advaitic Hinduism, which affirm the ultimately benign nature of the universe but which do not see the ultimate reality as a personal deity. So none of these theories can apply to all religion or therefore to religion as such. Durkheim and Freud don't seem to have known anything about Buddhism, nor did Marx. So the full picture is more complex than any of these theories recognize. But nevertheless there is an element of truth in them and it's truth about the human end of our awareness of the Transcendent, to use that term for the moment. But since the theories you've mentioned are rivals, each with its own proponents pushing it as the truth, which one do you go for?

DAVID: Well I suppose that in theory they could all be correct as explaining different aspects of religion. But basically I see religion as it lingers on in our own society today as pure wishful thinking: we would like there to be an omnipotent loving Being behind the universe in whom we can trust when life gets difficult, a greater power looking after us and making all well in the end. People would like that so much that they believe it, or at least sometimes believe it, and the churches rely on this, putting on a great show of authority, presenting the idea in universal images and impressive-sounding dogmas, with colourful liturgies and hierarchies which in the past people accepted uncritically. But today doubt has undermined that once immensely impressive structure. Science now makes a much stronger claim to authority, and through the eyes of the sciences the universe is nothing more than a vast, frigid emptiness, thinly contaminated with chemicals.

JOHN: So you say. But let me point to a basic mystery which the sciences can't explain. This is the very existence of the physical universe itself. Isn't that a mystery?

DAVID: No, that's the meaningless conundrum, Why is there something rather than nothing? It's meaningless because we can't even imagine what could count as an answer. We can't go behind the basic starting point that something *does* exist.

JOHN: No we can't, but that's not the question I'm asking. I'm asking Why does what exists take the specific form of *this* universe in which we find ourselves? The cosmologists tell us that it began with a 'big bang', the explosion of the minutest and densest possible particle some thirteen or so billion years ago into this still expanding universe of galaxies. Now if the big bang was the singularity we are told it was, an absolute beginning, what made it happen? Can something, however minute, suddenly come to be out of nothing? Can such a universe really be self-explanatory? What was there before the big bang, to bring it about?

DAVID: The answer is that there was no 'before the big bang' because time is a dimension of the physical universe. Time itself began with the big bang. So there's no question of there having to be a prior cause. The universe is a closed space-time system with no spatial or temporal outside.

JOHN: Yes, that's certainly one of the cosmological theories in the field today. But it still doesn't answer my question. Suppose that what exists *is* such a self-enclosed space-time continuum, an inside without an outside so to speak, we can still ask why that which exists takes this particular form. We can conceive of other forms it might have taken, and we both know that there are other cosmologists who do in fact propose different theories of its nature. The steady state theory has now been generally abandoned. But another possibility is that the total universe consists in a beginningless and endless series of expansions and contractions. So to describe it, whether in any of these or in some other way, is not to *explain* it. However you describe it, it still provokes the question, why does existence take *this* particular form? Isn't that just a basic mystery?

DAVID: There are indeed different theories, and so there *is* mystery in the sense that we don't know which of them, or some other yet to be developed, is correct. But this is typical of the way science progresses. Sooner or later the cosmologists will establish that one theory, either an existing one or a quite new one, fits their observations better than all the others, and is in fact the only form that a universe *could* take, and then we shall know why it has the particular character that it has. The point is that science as it advances will eventually settle the question. What is now a mystery will then no longer be mysterious.

JOHN: That, once again, is your assumption. I think, on the contrary, that the spheres of science and religion will never clash. The sciences are progressively discovering what the physical universe is composed of and how it works. But not why it exists at all in the form in which it does exist. That will always be a mystery from the point of view of the natural sciences, a mystery which scientists quite rightly ignore in doing their work in physics or chemistry or astronomy or whatever. It's outside their remit. In Wittgenstein's famous words, 'We feel that even if *all possible* scientific questions be answered, the problems of life have still not been touched at all.'[8]

DAVID: And I, alternatively, believe that all mysteries will eventually be resolved in the onward march of science. There is less and less room for God. In fact the idea that the universe is created to be the home for humanity and that an all-powerful God controls it for our benefit and intervenes miraculously in answer to prayer is simply not credible. Do you really think that God's existence can be proved?

JOHN: Let's discuss that next time.

2
Can God's Existence Be Proved?

DAVID: Do you claim that the existence of God can be proved?

JOHN: No, I don't think that any of the so-called theistic proofs succeed in proving that. Nor do most philosophers today. But they are nevertheless remarkable products of human reasoning. I think it would be worth our while to look at them again.

DAVID: I'm not a philosopher, as you know, so give me a tutorial on them.

JOHN: Okay. I suppose the most philosophically interesting is the ontological argument.

It began with Anselm, who lived in the medieval period, from 1033 to 1109. Though some scholars think that its essence can be found in Plato and in Augustine. But let's start with Anselm, who presents it very clearly and fully. He became Archbishop of Canterbury, and was a good guy in that he opposed the Crusades. He was a brilliant thinker, the most brilliant ever to have been AB of C.

DAVID: AB of C?

JOHN: Sorry. My private shorthand for the Archbishop of Canterbury. Anselm[1] said that by God we mean that than which no greater can be conceived, meaning by greater more perfect. If that than which no greater can be conceived exists only in the mind, it is not that than which no greater can be conceived. For if that than which no greater can be conceived exists in reality, and not only in the mind, it is greater (more perfect) than the same thing existing only in the mind. And so that than which no greater can be conceived must exist in reality as well as in our minds. Or, in other words, it is better to exist than not to exist, so that the best conceivable thing must exist – otherwise it would not be the best conceivable. This became known as the ontological argument. And although it looks at first sight like a verbal trick, and although it was challenged at the time by a monk called Gaunilo, it was many centuries before it was definitively refuted.

DAVID: And who eventually refuted it?

JOHN: It was Kant, the greatest philosopher of the modern period, who first published his *Critique of Pure Reason* in 1781. Anselm had treated existence as an attribute that something referred to can have or can lack. So that than which no more perfect can be conceived could either have the attribute of existing in reality, or lack it and thus exist only in the mind. But the most perfect conceivable thing must include the attribute of existence. However, Kant showed that existence is not an attribute. When we say that the concept of, say a horse, has the attribute of existence, so that horses exist, we are really saying that the concept of a horse is instantiated, that there are examples of it in the real world. So if you take the full concept of 'an-existing that-than-which-no-more-perfect-can-be-conceived' you can still ask, Is *that* concept instantiated? The mere fact of including existence in the definition of something does not guarantee that there are examples of it in reality.

DAVID: That sounds to me correct.

JOHN: Yes, like most philosophers I've long accepted Kant's critique of the argument, and Bertrand Russell's more recent way of putting the same point. And I also, incidentally, have my own critique of the second form of the argument that Charles Hartshorne and Norman Malcolm found in Anselm.[2] But we needn't go into that now.

DAVID: Okay. So what other philosophical arguments are there for the existence of God?

JOHN: We come down now to Thomas Aquinas, who lived from 1225 to 1274. He produced the first cause argument, that everything that comes into existence must have a cause and the cause of the universe must be other than the universe, and this cause is what we mean by God.

DAVID: Which you find persuasive?

JOHN: No. I don't see any reason why the universe *must* have a cause. It might just BE, as itself the ultimate reality. Something must just be, but this need not be God – it might be the universe itself. And again, even if the universe does have a cause, this might perfectly well not be a God in the religious sense – it might be an entirely impersonal, non-conscious, force.

DAVID: Yes, agreed again.

JOHN: And likewise the design argument, in its contemporary form of the 'anthropic principle', which claims that the basic constants necessary for the big bang to have produced galaxies, suns, planets, life, ourselves, constitutes intelligent design. As for these basic constants, to quote the astronomer, Martin Rees,

> The universe cannot have started off perfectly smooth and uniform. If it had, it would now contain hydrogen and helium gas so rarefied that there would have been less than one atom in each cubic meter everywhere. It would have been cold and dull: no galaxies, therefore no stars, no periodic table, no complexity, certainly no people. But because of the 'contrast enhancement' that's introduced by gravity during the expansion, even a slight initial uniformity could change all that. The amplitude of these nonuniformities can be described by a simple number Q – the energy difference between peaks and troughs in the density as a fraction of the total energy of the material. Q determines the scale of the biggest structures in the universe, with larger values of Q leading to a 'lumpier' universe. The computer models suggest that Q has to be about 0.00001 in order to account for present-day galaxies and clusters ... If Q were much smaller than 0.00001 galactic 'ecosystems' would never form: aggregations would take longer to develop, and their gravity would be too weak to retain gas. A very smooth universe would remain forever dark and featureless ... On the other hand, a rougher universe, with Q much larger than 0.00001, would be turbulent and violent. Lumps far larger than galaxies would condense early in its history. They would not fragment into stars: instead they would collapse into vast black holes ... [3]

This is what some call the fine-tuning of the universe which, they claim, requires a God to have done the fine-tuning.

DAVID: It strikes me that 'fine tuning' is a spin word, because it already applies a fine tuner. It smuggles God in surreptitiously. Don't you agree?

JOHN: As a matter of fact I do agree. Nor do I accept the argument even without that phrase. It's true that the necessary precision of the initial conditions is astonishing. So the argument is impressive, and I'm not surprised that many people are convinced by it. But it's weakened by there being another possible explanation of the data. This is the multiverse theory of innumerable universes, at least one of which happens to have all the basic constants that ours has, so that we are part of it as the only kind of universe we *could* be part of. Martin Rees (who is incidentally a very distinguished astronomer) claims that, 'the multiverse concept is already part of empirical science: we may already have intimations of other universes, and we could even draw inferences about them and the recipes that led to them. In an infinite ensemble, the existence of some universes that are seemingly fine-tuned to harbour life would occasion no surprise; our own cosmic habitat would plainly belong to this unusual subset'.[4] And again, even if the anthropic principle is accepted, it still doesn't lead to the God of religion. It could be an experiment by an all-powerful being who is not at all benign, or who has made a mistake, or any infant deity – as David Hume suggested – beginning to learn the art of creating.

DAVID: We seem to be agreed about that. Are there any more arguments for the existence of God?

JOHN: I think we ought to look at my friend Richard Swinburne's philosophically very precise version of something rather like the design argument. He presented this first in his book *The Existence of God*[5] thirty years ago. But more recently he has summarized and reformulated his argument in a shorter book *Is there a God?*[6] By God he means a being who is 'everlastingly omnipotent, omniscient, creator and sustainer of the universe, perfectly good, and a source of moral obligation' (18), and God has all these attributes essentially – that is, without any of them he would not be God. Further, God 'is a personal being – that is, in some sense *a person'* (4). Swinburne also holds that God, as a moral being, has duties and obligations, for 'some moral truths are moral truths quite independent of the will of God' (15).

Why should we believe that such a being exists? Swinburne puts it this way. The existence of the universe needs an explanation, for 'It is extraordinary that there should exist anything at all. Surely the most natural state of affairs is simply nothing: no universe, no God, nothing' (pp. 48–9). But since there are things, this fact demands an explanation. And

> That theory of ultimate explanation is most likely to be the true one, which is the simplest theory that predicts the observable phenomena when one would not otherwise expect to find them ... Theism claims that every other object that exists is caused to exist and kept in existence by just one substance, God ... It is a hallmark of a simple explanation to postulate few causes. There could in this respect be no simpler explanation than one which postulated only one cause. (pp. 41 and 43)

In other words, the existence of the universe would not be expected, but theism predicts it, in the sense that a God, and indeed a good God, is likely, as Swinburne later argues, to have created it.

He then points to the almost incredible complexity and yet uniformity of behaviour in the world. For example, the law of gravity applies everywhere. But there is also the 'fine-tuning' of the universe, the very precise initial state in which it must have been to produce order and life. Indeed 'many eighteenth-century writers argued that there was no reason to suppose chance would throw up such beautiful organization, whereas God was able to do so and had abundant reason to do so – in the goodness ... of embodied animals and humans. Here their existence, they argued, was good evidence of the existence of God. I believe', Swinburne adds, 'this argument ... to be correct' (56–7). He concludes,

> The simple hypothesis of theism leads us to expect all the phenomena I have been describing with some reasonable degree of probability. God being omnipotent is able to produce a world orderly in these respects. And he has good reason to choose to do so: a world containing human beings is a good thing. Persons have experiences, and thoughts, and can make choices, and their choices can make big differences to themselves, to others, and to the inanimate world. God, being perfectly good, is generous. He wants to share ... (52)

There is more in Swinburne's book (and in his many other books) than this. He also tackles the problem of evil, and shows how the existence of God can explain miracles, revelation and religious experience.

DAVID: And you find this persuasive?

JOHN: No, I don't.

DAVID: Why? I wonder if it's for the same as my reasons.

JOHN: Well first, Swinburne says that 'he [God] is the ultimate brute fact which explains everything else' (19). And it is true that, if there is the kind of God that Swinburne describes, his existence would explain everything else – with the possible exception of the fact of evil in the form of pain and suffering and wickedness, which is something that we must ourselves discuss later. But why should not the physical universe itself be the ultimate brute fact, its character explaining everything within it? For a creator is not the simplest possible explanation of the universe. An even simpler one is that the physical universe is uncreated, eternally existing – this being the ultimate brute fact.

DAVID: Yes, these are my objection too. So we both accept that there are no sound philosophical arguments for the existence of God.

JOHN: There are yet other attempted proofs or arguments. But I don't think any of them is strong enough for us to need to look at them now.

DAVID: Now you are left with no reason to believe in God; so obviously you should become an atheist like me!

JOHN: I would if the kind of God we've been discussing was the kind of God I believe in. So I think we need now to ask what we mean by God.

3
What Do We Mean by God?

JOHN: Let me ask you first, What kind of God is it that you, as an atheist, do not believe in?

DAVID: I mean what I suppose most people mean: an all-powerful divine being who knows everything, is infinitely wise, good and loving, and who is the creator and ruler of the universe, and who intervenes from time to time on earth, either on his own initiative or in answer to prayer, as recounted in the Bible. But I don't believe for a moment that any such being exists.

JOHN: And nor do I.

DAVID: Oh, you don't! So you've come over to the Humanist camp?

JOHN: No, not at all. What I call the Transcendent or the ultimate reality is not the God you describe, and that for two reasons, one religious and the other philosophical.

DAVID: The philosophical one being … ?

JOHN: There are huge philosophical debates about whether such concepts as omnipotence and omniscience are logically viable. There are discussions about such conundrums as Can an omnipotent person make something so heavy that even he cannot lift it? Can an omniscient person know everything, including the future decisions of free beings? But I want to focus on a question that is prior to these, namely, does the idea of an *infinite person* make sense? We know what we mean by a person because we are ourselves persons. And to be a person is to be a particular person, distinct from other persons, with our own boundaries. When two people are interacting with each other as persons, this is only possible because each of them has his or her own individual borders – otherwise they would not be two distinct persons. In other words, personhood is essentially finite.

DAVID: Yes, I once put essentially that point to a theologian and his response was that God is not *a* person, but that God is personal.

JOHN: Yes, I know. I've often heard or read that myself. But I'm sure you'll agree that this is merely to dodge the problem. What would it be to be personal but not a person?

DAVID: What indeed? But I can imagine what the theologians will say: that if God is not personal he, or it, must be sub-personal, lower than ourselves!

JOHN: Yes, I've heard that too. But what I am calling the Transcendent is beyond all our human concepts, including personal, impersonal, sub-personal. We're going to come to that later, I hope.

DAVID: Alright, we'll look at that later. In the meantime, what is your religious reason for rejecting the standard concept of God?

JOHN: Well, the religious value of the idea is that we can have a personal relationship with the all-powerful God, so that we can ask him or her to help us with our personal problems, and the world with its much bigger problems. God can be 'a very present help in time of trouble'. In other words, it is assumed that God can and does answer prayer when he or she so decides. In church we pray for wisdom for our rulers, for peace on earth, for those who are starving in Africa or elsewhere, for justice for the persecuted and downtrodden, and so on – a long list of the world's problems. And often when people have escaped from some serious danger, or when they've experienced some great good fortune, they thank God for it. Often of course that's just a form of words. But many genuinely devout people mean it literally. To pinpoint the difficulty, suppose there's a car crash in the road outside, three of the four people in the car being killed but the fourth remaining 'miraculously' unhurt. Suppose the survivor then thanks God for saving her, really meaning what she says. She would be forgetting that if it was, so to speak, okay from God's point of view to intervene miraculously on earth, then God must not only have decided to save her but also decided *not* to save the other three. What then becomes of God's universal love? Why does he or she not intervene to prevent terrible events all over the world? Why be so selective? The age-old problem of God and evil now comes to the fore.

DAVID: Hear, hear! I completely agree with you. I've often made the same point myself when arguing with religious friends. Prayer, in the sense of asking God to do this or that, and God then deciding whether or not to oblige, does not make sense for a rational and loving God. Prayer – we're talking about what is called intercessory prayer, prayer for oneself or other people – requires an arbitrary God.

JOHN: Except that it all depends on what we mean by prayer.

DAVID: How do you mean?

JOHN: Well I believe that at an unconscious level we are all linked together in a common network in which we are potentially affecting one another all the time by our thoughts and even more by our emotions. I say 'potentially' because we all have screening mechanisms to protect our individual autonomy – without that we'd be continually flooded by others' thoughts and emotions. The extent to which we are sensitive to others in this way varies from person to person. But in the kind of prayer – if indeed you want to call it prayer – that I'm talking about we focus our thought and concern very concretely on someone we know, someone whom we know is anxious or depressed or afraid or confused or in a state of anger or resentment, or indeed who is ill, and visualize them and think positively of them in a better state. I strongly suspect that our thought, reinforced by compassion, love, well-wishing, may actually have a positive effect on them. And of course also strengthening and encouraging other people who are not in any particular negative state. It's what the Buddhists call loving-kindness meditation on behalf of someone.

DAVID: But does this actually work?

JOHN: Yes, it does sometimes seem to.

DAVID: Even with physical illnesses?

JOHN: Yes, if there is a psycho-somatic element in the illness, as there often is. Then our thoughts affect the unwell person's mind, which in turn affects their body.

DAVID: Well, I'm not going to say that all this is impossible. Though whether there is any such a thing as mind-to-mind causation – extra-sensory perception or telepathy – seems to me extremely doubtful. However, returning to your own religion, I can see that it is turning out to be fairly complex and a long way removed from what people get in the churches.

JOHN: Yes, it is.

DAVID: Particularly when you don't believe that there is a God.

JOHN: Actually, in a sense I do. Or rather, I think there are probably many gods with a small g. That is, there probably are higher personal beings with whom we can be in a personal relationship. They are what the Christian tradition calls angels, the Hindus call gods, and the Buddhists call *devas*. They are not infinite, whether in power, knowledge, or anything else; they're not the creator of the universe; but they are higher beings than ourselves whom we can address in prayer and by whom we can be influenced.

DAVID: 'Higher'?

JOHN: Yes, meaning more spiritually mature than us, living in a more powerful awareness of the ultimate reality.

DAVID: But how do you think these supposed higher beings influence us?

JOHN: Through this psychic, meaning mental, network I spoke about.

DAVID: So, in Christian terms, you think there are angels, but no God with a capital G?

JOHN: In Christian terms, yes. Though that's less than half the story.

DAVID: So you think that the capital G Gods of Judaism, Christianity and Islam, and any other ones, are really finite angelic beings?

JOHN: It's more complex than that. On the one hand, I believe that when in prayer, or indeed in any other context, someone is conscious of being in an I–Thou relationship with what they take to be God – with all the traditional omni-attributes – they may well really be in relationship with someone, but that someone is a *deva* – to use the eastern term in order to shed the image of angels in white robes and wings.

DAVID: And how would you defend that to your fellow Christians – who are nearly all much more orthodox than you?

JOHN: Indeed they are. I point out that one cannot logically claim to be conscious of being in a personal relationship with an omnipotent, omniscient, infinitely good and loving being.

DAVID: Why not?

JOHN: Because one could never know that the being one is in a personal relationship with is omni-anything. You could experience that he or she is *very* powerful, *very* knowing, *very* good and loving, but not infinitely so. Infinity goes beyond any possible experience. It was David Hume who said that if you have a balance, and you can see one side but not the other, and you put a ten pounds weight on the end you can see, and it's outweighed by something on the other end, you know that that something weighs more than ten pounds, but not that it is infinitely heavy.

DAVID: Yes, and of course he was obviously right. So does this mean that the Catholics who pray to a saint or the Virgin Mary, who they know to be finite beings, may be behaving perfectly sensibly?

JOHN: Yes, I suppose it does – though that hadn't occurred to me. They may well be in the same boat as the village Hindus who pray to their local god.

DAVID: And may we all have our own guardian angel?

JOHN: For all I know, yes. But of course I don't know.

DAVID: Okay, now going back a step, I think you said that worshippers 'may well be' in a real personal relationship with someone. What is the force of that *may* be?

JOHN: I certainly don't want to say that whenever someone believes they are talking to a higher being whom they call God they are always in contact with a real being. There are religious as well as non-religious hallucinations.

DAVID: Yes indeed. And my question is going to be whether the other more impressive cases are equally delusions. But at the moment I want to know what for you is the status of the God of monotheism. Is he or she one of the *devas* pretending to be infinite and ultimate?

JOHN: No. To start with, we can't speak of *the* God of monotheism because the deity worshipped within

Judaism, Christianity and Islam is in each case describably different. The God of the Hebrew scriptures – let's use the name Adonai, 'my Lord', used in Jewish worship – exists in an indissoluble covenant relationship with the Jewish people. He is part of their history and they are part of his. And he develops in the course of their history, as reflected in the Hebrew scriptures, from the violent warrior god of a particular tribe, leading them in battle and conquest, to the moral deity who both punishes and rewards his people according to their behaviour, and finally to the universal Lord of heaven and earth. Likewise the God of Christianity started as the heavenly Father whom Jesus taught his followers to worship, but developed in the thought of the Church into the Holy Trinity of Father, Son and Holy Spirit, three in one and one in three. So the God of the Christian Church is trinitarian whereas the Jewish God is unitarian, as also is the Allah – which is Arabic, as you probably know, for God – of Islam. But the Qur'anic Allah has a different earthly history from the Jewish Adonai. The two stories overlap in that many of the great figures of the Torah – Abraham, Moses and so on – are also great prophets in the Qur'an. But, at the same time, Allah helps the Muslim but not the Jewish community in battle. And so Adonai (or Jahweh), the Holy Trinity and Allah are not simply three different names for the same deity. They are names for describably different deities, each of whom is said to be the creator and ruler of heaven and earth. So there is no *the* God of monotheism but three different and overlapping monotheisms.

DAVID: Precisely. So according to you there are at least three Gods – and a great many more when we include all the thousands of local and tribal gods of India and Africa and elsewhere. And as well as the Gods, there are also the non-personal Absolutes of some of the eastern religions, such as Buddhism. The supporters of each claim that theirs is the true ultimate reality. But obviously only one at most can be, so that to affirm one is by implication to reject all the others. So each is rejected by a majority vote! Or, as our friend David Hume put it, if a judge hears several witnesses each of whom contradicts the others, he will disregard them all.[1] And this is what I do with the witness of the religions. Each contradicts the others, so I dismiss them all.

JOHN: And given the traditional concept of God, I don't blame you. But the whole situation changes within the quite different framework of the philosophy of religion I'm advocating.

DAVID: Which is what I want to get at. But before we go any further, it's clear that its central pillar is the reality of the Transcendent, and I'm sure you know that there are Christian thinkers today who undercut the entire discussion by advocating religion without transcendence. I think we ought at this point to look at what they say. Agreed?

JOHN: Yes, by all means.

4
Religion without Transcendence?

DAVID: I'm interested in the possibility of doing without transcendence altogether, while retaining a basically religious world-view. If people like you can accept this, it will make our discussion and disagreements unnecessary. A friend of mine, Donwi, who used to be found sometimes in Cambridge and sometimes in Swansea, is a notable advocate of that position. Let's ask him to expound it.

JOHN: Yes, please go ahead, Donwi.

DONWI:[1] Okay. A growing number of Christians today, including myself, are seeing religion as a wholly this-world affair, a matter of how we live now. We don't have to believe in any transcendent divine reality. We're content with this world and our life within it. When people speak about God, meaning an infinite loving Person who created the universe, what they are really referring to, according to us – some of us in the Sea of Faith movement, for example – is our own human ideals of love and goodness and the demands that these make on us. The personal God is a projected personification of our human ideals. It's 'a unifying symbol that eloquently personifies and represents to us everything that spirituality requires of us'.[2] It's because we have high and demanding ideals that religion exists, but the 'word "God" does not refer to an entity that is supposed to exist quite apart from the practice of religion'.[3] And as for divine creation, 'Talk of creation expresses what it feels like to have been re-made through faith',[4] nothing to do with bringing the universe into existence. In fact the whole gamut of religious language – not only Christian, or even theistic, but Buddhist and Hindu as well – should be taken in a non-realist way which creates no issues between science and religion.

JOHN: Yes, and of course I know that this non-realist position is held by quite a number of people.

DAVID: Let me intervene at this point to ask you both to clarify for me what you mean by realism and non-realism.

JOHN: Yes, in this context of the discussion of religion, realism holds that there is a transcendent reality of some kind, of which the religions speak, and non-realism, and also anti-realism – which is simply aggressive non-realism – denies this. Right Donwi?

DONWI: Yes, that's right.

JOHN: Okay. This is in fact a contemporary version of Ludwig Feuerbach in the early nineteenth century. He spoke of a 'religious atheism'[5] according to which 'The divine being is nothing else than the human being, or, rather, the human nature purified, freed from the limits of the individual man, made objective – i.e. contemplated and revered as another, a distinct being',[6] so that 'the divine love is only human love made objective, affirming itself'.[7]

In contrast to that I see religion as involving, as well of course as morality, a conception of the structure of the universe – the totality of reality and not only its physical aspect – a structure which forms the basis of what I call the cosmic optimism of the great traditions.

DONWI: You mean including some kind of life after death, leading to some sort of heavenly existence?

JOHN: Yes, except that I don't accept the traditional Christian ideas of heaven and hell – but we can come to that later.

DONWI: To me, the real meaning of eternal life is an 'eternal' *quality* of life that's possible for us now, not an endless prolongation of life after death. 'Eternity is not an extension of this present life, but a mode of judging it. Eternity is not *more* life, but this life seen under certain moral and religious modes of thought.'[8] Any idea of an ultimate bringing of good out of evil in a further life or lives beyond this one, such as I know John talks about, is simply a comforting delusion. I can quote scripture in support of this: 'this is eternal life, that they know thee the only true God, and Jesus Christ whom thou hast sent' (John 17:3). It's a matter of living now under the claim of our highest ideals.

JOHN: I don't think either of us really believes that you can settle the big issues with a biblical quote. In any case that quote, as you've interpreted it, certainly does not represent the central New Testament view, because the teaching of Jesus is full of the consequences of what we do now for our future beyond death. But surely, quite apart from the New Testament, it's a simple mistake to think that eternal life has to be *either* a present quality of life *or* the prolongation of life beyond death. Why can't it be both, as the continued movement towards that quality beyond this life?

DONWI: Yes, no doubt it could be both if both existed, but in fact there is no prolongation beyond this life. The only eternal life available has to be a quality of life on earth here and now. And in varying degrees and ways we can all attain it.

JOHN: The eternal quality of life you're talking about is a state of moral goodness, isn't it, and a fulfilment of the highest potentialities of our human nature? You speak of varying degrees of this, but surely to count as the *eternal* quality of life, as distinguished from something less, that degree of goodness must be pretty high. But can we all attain that? Indeed, can any of us attain it in this life?

DONWI: Yes, of course we can. It's up to us, each of us.

JOHN: It's easy for those of us who have been fortunate in the circumstances of our lives, as we three have, to think that, and even to make some beginning of an approach to it ourselves. We were born into loving families, with a reasonable income, in a highly civilized society, and have benefited from a well-developed educational system. But what about the baby who dies at a few days old? What about the boy who is born in a teeming poverty-stricken slum and is knifed or shot in a gang war and dies at the age of 15? What about the girl who is raped and strangled at the age of 16? What about the hundreds of millions who are living on less than a dollar a day, and the many among them who are deeply anxious all the time, faced with possible starvation for themselves and their families; and those – a vast number today – whose lives are cut short by AIDS and other diseases; and those living in constant fear of death in the brutality of civil or international war; those exploited or enslaved; those lacking education and any opportunity to develop their intellectual and cultural and social potentialities? Surely, to say that they are all free to attain to the eternal quality of life is a cruel joke – like saying that everyone in a poverty-stricken society is free to become a millionaire. The fact is that, whereas you and I have been lucky in life's lottery, very many millions of our fellow human beings have not. And, according to the naturalistic picture their unfulfilled potential must remain eternally unfulfilled. Surely when you take a global view that overall picture is a very bleak one.

DAVID: This is getting pretty heavy! A lot of what you say may well be true. But you can't blame naturalism for it. If there's a God you must blame him – or her.

JOHN: That presupposes a particular concept of God which I myself don't share, as you know from our earlier discussions. But you don't think there *is* a God, or any other reality beyond the material. You are a materialist, aren't you, believing that only matter exists?

DAVID: We prefer to call it physicalism.

JOHN: Okay, physicalism. But it's the belief that nothing but the physical universe exists. Okay?

DAVID: Yes.

JOHN: And the point I'm making is that your picture of the human situation is a desperately grim and depressing one. I hasten to add that this doesn't show that it's false – I want to make that clear – but I think you should be unhappily conscious that if naturalism is true it is very, very bad news for humanity as a whole.

DONWI: It doesn't have to be. It's up to us, the human family, to overcome those evils. Almost all the things you have pointed to are humanly created and could be humanly changed. This is the challenge of being human. The answer is not pie in the sky when you die, but becoming committed to finding creative solutions here and now.

JOHN: Needless to say, I'm all for finding practical solutions now to the world's problems. But your philosophy is not going to be good news concerning the hundreds of millions who have already lived and died, or for the millions now living who find themselves in terrible conditions and can see those conditions for the most part continuing into the future. It's always been up to humanity to solve its own problems, and happily some progress is being made, much more now than in the past, but still there has been and still is a vast waste of the human potential. And my point is that if you are right there is no hope for all of those who have lived and died, and very little for millions now living, and an uncertain future for those yet to come, so that on a genuinely global view the human situation is bleak in the extreme. We now face the dangers flowing from global warming, from overpopulation and from the possibility of nuclear war, as well as the ever present fact of extreme poverty with all its consequences. As Terry Eagleton has written, 'Whatever they call themselves, the hard-nosed realists who claim that there is no need for another world clearly have not been reading the newspapers.'[9]

DONWI: Well maybe we have to accept that this is just how the world is.

JOHN: Maybe we do. But what I'm pressing you to see is what a bleak picture naturalism, or humanism, or materialism paints. I wish you would emulate the frankness and clarity of vision of the really tough-minded humanists, such as Bertrand Russell. You remember this famous passage of his:

> That Man is the product of causes which had no previ-sion of the end they were achieving; that his origins, his growth, his hopes and fears, his loves and his beliefs, are but the outcome of accidental collocations of atoms; that no fire, no heroism, no intensity of thought and feeling, can preserve an individual beyond the grave; that all the labours of the ages, all the devotion, all the inspiration, all the noonday brightness of human genius, are destined to extinction in the vast death of the solar system, and that the whole temple of Man's achievement must inevi-tably be buried beneath the debris of a universe in ruins – all these things, if not quite beyond dispute, are yet so nearly certain, that no philosophy that rejects them can hope to stand. Only within the scaffolding of these truths, only on the firm foundation of unyielding despair, can the soul's habitation henceforth be safely built.[10]

As I've already said, that this picture of our human situation is so utterly bleak does not, unfortunately, show that it is false. Things could be as bad as that.

It could be that human existence is a brief moment in one minute corner of the universe, lasting for just a flash of time on the cosmic scale, with the universe then going on as it did before as though we had never existed. If so, our life has whatever meaning we can individually give it, and for those who have been lucky in life's lottery it can have a truly rich and satisfying meaning. But to base our philosophy on ourselves only, ignoring the hundreds of millions who are much less fortunate, would be an 'I'm all right, Jack' elitism. I think you ought – without abandoning your naturalism – to be acutely aware of its terrible implications for humanity as a whole. I find that in Russell and some of the other philosophers and scientists, but hardly ever among the non-realist theologians.

DONWI: 'Elitism' is a harsh word. I agree that there are great variations in the human condition around the world. There are those who are fortunate and those who are unfortunate in what you call the lottery of life. But even the child who's born and then dies a few days later of disease or starvation has shared a little tiny bit in the human story. And even those who live in miserable conditions – half-starving, or wickedly exploited for others' profit, or with the wasting disease of AIDS, and so on – even they have their share of life and love and beauty, even if it's often a very small share. It's remarkable what fortitude people often show even amid terrible poverty, and it's inspiring to see how they often care for one another even in the direst circumstances. We shouldn't write off any life as not worth living. All human life is good in some degree, even though the degrees do, as you say, vary enormously.

JOHN: Frankly, although that's true I don't think it saves the naturalistic picture from being deeply bad news for humanity as a whole. The fact is that a world in which undernourishment, lacking the proteins for proper development of the body, widespread starvation, oppression, disease, young lives cut off by violent death, is a world in which the human potential will never be fulfilled except to a very slight extent for a vast number of human beings. If this present life in which some of us are so very lucky and others, a great many, are so very unlucky, if this is the whole of the human story, it's much more a tragedy than a comedy.

DAVID: Yes, this may perhaps be true. But surely all this is just as much a problem for a religious understanding of the universe. So let's come back to your own philosophy. Where do you start?

5
Religious Experience

JOHN: Where do I start? I start at ground level, so to speak, with religious experience.

DAVID: You mean seeing visions and hearing voices and that sort of thing?

JOHN: Including some of that, yes, but much more. And also excluding some of that and much more. The trouble with the term 'religious experience' is that it covers such a wide range, from the sublime to the ridiculous to the downright dangerous. But let's start with the religious, or numinous, or mystical experiences of ordinary people.

DAVID: Do ordinary people have such experiences?

JOHN: Yes, about a third of people, at least once in their lives, according to several quite large surveys in the USA and Britain.[1] Commenting on these surveys David Hay says:

> What we found was that over a third of all adults in Britain would claim to have had experience of this kind. Generally speaking, women are rather more likely to claim these experiences than men, in the ratio of four to

three. As one moves up the social scale, more people will talk about religious experience; also, the more education people have, the more likely they are to talk about their experience. The happier people are, and the older they are, the more likely they are to claim experience. Most interesting of all, those who report religious experience are more likely than others to be in a good state of psychological well-being.[2]

And of course there may be many more than those who have come to the attention of the researchers. This was done mainly by the Alister Hardy Research Centre, and those who happened to read their newspaper ads inviting those who had had such experiences to contact it must be a very small proportion of the total population. So I think it's reasonable to assume that we should think of a far higher proportion than a third.

DAVID: I suppose so. But give me some examples from those who are known.

JOHN: Let's look at what are called peak experiences, or altered states of consciousness, or, in the formula of the Alister Hardy Research Centre, 'modern religious and other transcendent experiences'.

DAVID: This Research Centre being?

JOHN: It was set up in 1969 by Sir Alister Hardy when Professor of Zoology at Oxford, to collect reports of these 'transcendent experiences', and it's now based at the University of Wales at Lampeter. Several writers have drawn on the collection.[3] Most of those in Britain who have responded to the Alister Hardy Centre's advertisements have had a Protestant background – though often much more in the background than the foreground. This may be because the term 'religious experience' is a characteristically Protestant term, liable to sound too individualistic within the generally more sacramentally and ecclesiastically oriented Catholicism. In this respect, much depends on how the questions are phrased. However, Catholic sociological researchers in the United States, Greeley and McCready, also found much the same proportion of people, around a third, reporting some form of religious experience, and also noted 'an association between religious experience, well-being, and concern for the well-being of other people'.[4]

DAVID: Okay. So let's have some examples.

JOHN: Let's start with the group of those that occur outdoors and involve a sense of the 'goodness' of existence, linked with a sense of union with the environment. For example,

> I was standing alone on the edge of a low cliff overlooking a small valley leading to the sea. It was late afternoon or early evening and there were birds swooping in the sky – possibly swallows. Suddenly my mind 'felt' as though it had changed gear or switched into another view of things. I still saw the birds and everything around me but instead of standing looking at them, I *was* them and they were me. I was also the sea and the sound of the sea and the grass and sky. Everything and I were the same, all one. It was the most peaceful and 'right' feeling imaginable and I knew without any smallest doubt that everything happened for a reason, a good reason, and fitted into everything else, like an arch with all the bricks supporting each other and their cornerstone

without cement, just by their being there. I was filled, swamped, with happiness and peace. Everything was RIGHT. I don't know how long it lasted, probably only a second or two.[5]

Or another,

One day years ago I went for a walk in the fields with my dog. My mind suddenly started thinking about the beauty around me, and I considered the marvellous order and timing of the growth of each flower, herb and the abundance of all the visible growth going on around. I remember thinking 'Here is mind'. Then we had to get over a style and suddenly I was confronted with a bramble bush which was absolutely laden with black glistening fruit. And the impact of that, linked with my former reasoning, gave me a great feeling of ecstasy. For a few moments I really did feel at one with the Universe or the Creative power we recognise. I know it was a feeling of oneness with something outside my self, and also within. I must have been confronted with the source of all being, whatever one should call it. I have often told my friends about it, though it seems too sacred to talk about. The experience has never been forgotten. It was quite electric and quite unsought.[6]

DAVID: Well I've also often been moved by the beauties of nature, probably just as much as you, but I don't feel any need to suppose that there's a mysterious 'presence' or 'spirit' within it or behind it. Surely, one can appreciate the glory of a sunset, or a shining blackberry bush, without thinking of it in that mystical way.

JOHN: Yes, indeed one can. But in these reports a recurrent theme is the sense that the universe is benign or friendly, that basically all is well, and hence a sense of peacefulness and the conviction that there is ultimately nothing to worry about. Here are a few of the many examples in the Maxwell and Tschuden volume taken from the Alister Hardy Centre files:

> I was part of something bigger and absolutely beyond me. My problems and my life didn't matter at all because I was such a tiny part of a great whole. I felt a tremendous relief. (p. 47)

> I feel a lot more peaceful and happier within myself. (49)

> Even though the experience lasted perhaps a couple of minutes, it was so peaceful and joyous. I felt lighter. (51)

> The feeling was indescribable ... it was blissful, uplifting. (53)

> I later faced an operation quite calmly because I realized it really didn't matter now whether I lived or died, because everything was taken care of and everything was for the best. (55)

> I felt the peace of God, which does indeed pass all understanding. I have never lost that inner peace. (94)

> I will never forget that moment of absolute peace and certainty. (95)

> suddenly this calm, peaceful feeling took over. (147)

> I became aware of the goodness of everything. (151)

These are typical examples of experiences in which many people participate. And what is most significant about them is that they answer the question that Einstein said was the most important question we can ask, 'Is the universe friendly or not?'

DAVID: Yes, I can see that for those who have such experiences they must be extremely important.

JOHN: Indeed. And there are other examples of a different kind and usually lesser intensity coming from participation in religious rituals. We'll come presently to forms of experience in which fewer people participate, but first, still at this everyday level, do you not sense a non-physical dimension to life in the awareness of goodness in our fellow human beings – unsolicited acts of kindness and compassion, the response of sympathy with someone in great distress, unselfish and sometimes courageous acts of service to the community, dedicated commitment to creating social justice, examples of heroic self-sacrifice for others ... ? Surely, here we are aware of values that are real and yet transcend our purely physical existence.

DAVID: Yes indeed, but again I see nothing religious here. I'm also deeply impressed and inspired by moral heroes and extraordinary acts of goodness. They reveal something about human nature, but they don't in any way demand a religious interpretation. What they reveal about human nature may be no more than the evolutionary value of altruism in the sense of acts which benefit others at some cost to the individual. There are many examples of this in animal life: for example,

[I]n numerous bird species, a breeding pair receives help in raising its young from other 'helper' birds who protect the nest from predators, feed the fledgling birds and more. Vampire bats regularly donate blood to other members of their group who have failed to feed themselves, thus altruistically ensuring they do not starve. Velvet monkeys give alarm calls to warn fellow monkeys of the presence of predators, even though in doing so they attract attention to themselves, increasing their personal chance of being attacked.[7]

And the evolutionary reason for this, according to the kin selection theory, is the preservation of the genes which the individual has in common with its relatives. At times the individual animal can do this better by protecting the group than by protecting itself. And it has in fact been found that 'birds are much more likely to help relatives raise their young than they are to help unrelated breeding pairs. Similarly, several studies of monkeys have shown that altruistic actions tend to be directed towards close kin.'[8] And we humans are just further along the same evolutionary scale as the monkeys. So altruism may have a purely natural explanation which does not involve any sense of transcendence. Nietzsche was about right when he said that morality is the herd instinct in the individual.

JOHN: That theory may possibly explain altruism within a kinship group, but surely working for justice for people far beyond the kinship group, working to 'make poverty history', working for the sake of the human community globally, cannot be explained in this way?

DAVID: No, granted. But another biological principle may also come into play – reciprocal altruism, one individual helping another with the expectation that the other will later help him or her. Thus 'Bats are more likely to share blood with those who have shared with them in the past than with those who have not. So a bat that selfishly refuses to share with others will do worse in the long run.'[9] This may be the other purely natural factor within human altruism. You'll remember that this is Richard Dawkins's biological account of morality in *The God Delusion*[10] – its twin pillars are kinship and reciprocity.

JOHN: Reciprocal altruism no doubt applies quite often on a small scale, between neighbours and friends and relatives, and even on a larger scale between villages and tribes. But reciprocity doesn't lead you to give money to help the victims of a tsunami at the other end of the earth, whom you will never meet. Again, what of the reformers and liberators whose lives evoke our awe and challenge us to a greater concern for humanity. I don't think that any selfish concern can cover Mahatma Gandhi, or Martin Luther King, or Helda Camera, or Oscar Romero, or Nelson Mandela, or a great number of others who have lived, and often given their lives, in the service of humanity.

DAVID: No, perhaps not. But at least you'll agree that the things you've been pointing to don't amount to any kind of proof of the transcendent reality you talk about?

JOHN: Agreed. And I didn't refer to them to remove the ambiguity of the universe that I was arguing for earlier. The various forms of religious experience can be given a naturalistic interpretation by those who do not participate in them, leaving that ambiguity intact.

But let me emphasize the common feature that occurs in the great majority of the kind of case of which I've just give you some examples. These are that the experiences, although they take a great variety of forms, are basically an awareness of the ultimate 'goodness' of existence, an awareness which removes fears and anxieties. You may remember that when Einstein was asked, 'What is the most important question you can ask?' he replied, 'Is the universe friendly or not?' An experience which makes someone answer Yes is usually a moment of intense happiness. And often it affects the rest of their lives. Though I must add that there are also some exceptions in which there is a terrifying sense of evil. But typically it is a sense of the rightness and goodness of the universe.

DAVID: Yes, and I don't doubt that these people did have the experiences that they describe. The question is whether they have unconsciously created them for themselves, as wish fulfilment. But tell me, were these accounts all written soon after the experiences?

JOHN: No, usually not, because they were mostly only recorded in response to an advertisement from the Alister Hardy Centre inviting people who had had any kind of 'transcendent' experience to report it to them. David Hay says, 'Something about the private interview situation seemed to give people permission to speak of a long-suppressed experience. In our 1986 national survey, as many as 40 percent of people claiming experience said that they had never told anyone else about it.'[11] Many of those who responded had only had one such experience, though many others had had several, but it had been for them unforgettable and sometimes such as to change their outlook on life. They often welcomed the opportunity to share their experience in this way. They hadn't wanted to talk about it before for fear of being thought peculiar or 'spooky'. The Centre reports are all published anonymously, although the Centre itself has the names and addresses and such details as age, gender and occupation.

DAVID: And presumably the time gap between the experience itself and their recording it in writing means that conscious or unconscious interpretation may well have crept in.

JOHN: Yes. I think one can see that in some of the reports. And not only is there sometimes a conscious interpretation embodied in the report, but more basically the experience itself will always be structured by the experiencer's conceptual system, including religious beliefs. But *all* conscious experience without exception – including our ordinary sense experience – is structured by our innate and acquired conceptual systems, and if in these religious experiences people are being affected by transcendent reality, this also will come to consciousness in the ways made possible by their religious or other concepts. So we find that the different conceptualities of different religions produce different conscious experiences: for example, whereas a Christian may have a vision of Jesus or the Virgin Mary, a Hindu may have a vision of Krishna.[12] But this doesn't vitiate the central feature that pervades so many of them, expressed in many different ways, of a sense of the benign or friendly nature of reality, and the often transforming effect of this awareness on their lives.

DAVID: That is striking, I agree. But without having had any such experience oneself it's difficult to know what to make of them. Do you know anyone who has had this kind of experience?

JOHN: Yes, several, including myself.

DAVID: Indeed! Tell me about your own.

JOHN: I'll tell you about one, though there have been several. I use a form of meditation learned from a Buddhist monk, Nyanaponika, in Sri Lanka more than thirty years ago. On this occasion several years ago now, I had been doing this, sitting at my desk after breakfast. When I opened my eyes everything was different, in two ways. Instead of there being me here and the surrounding world there, apart from me – shelves of books in the room and trees and sky outside seen through the window – I was part of a single indivisible whole. And the totality of which I was part, not just what I could see, was such that there couldn't possibly be anything to be afraid of or to be anxious about. It was extraordinarily joyous, liberating and uplifting and such that I can only use hackneyed words like wonderful, marvellous, sublime, even though for me it only lasted a very short time, perhaps less than a minute – it's hard to say. I think myself that the awareness of the 'friendliness' of the universe was the most important aspect of it, as it seems to have been for so many of those in the Alister Hardy Centre files.

DAVID: I notice you speak of the universe as being *friendly*. This sounds to me like an example of the interpretation we were talking about a moment ago. Only persons can be friendly, so that by implication you're importing God into the experience. But the universe revealed to us by the sciences, with its millions of millions of stars scattered through immense space, forming and then later disintegrating, is completely impersonal, neither friendly nor unfriendly, just totally unaware of us and our feelings. The universe is completely indifferent to us.

JOHN: So far as the physical universe is concerned, yes. And, as you say, 'friendly' and 'benign' normally imply personality and I don't want to imply that the universe has any personal qualities. Likewise 'good'. But we do quite often stretch the words metaphorically beyond any implication of personality. We speak, for example, of something being user-friendly, and of a benign climate. Likewise goodness – if you overcook spinach you take all the goodness out of it, and fruit and vegetables are *good* for our health. It's this sort of metaphorical sense that all these reports, including my own, are using. And it's crucial that I am using the word 'universe' to refer to the *total* situation in which we are and of which we are a part. Clearly in experiencing this as benign, removing all occasion for fears or anxieties, one is being aware of much more than the physical universe. So I think that the experience which has come to so many people is of a reality, indeed of Reality with a capital R, which both transcends matter and also pervades it and is encountered through it.

DAVID: Reality or, of course, illusion! Aren't there any cases in the records that suggest even to you that the experiencer is unconsciously deluding him or herself?

JOHN: There are indeed. Here's my favourite example:

> After I felt the call of God to trust Him for everything I was in the RAF as an aircraft mechanic. After a short

time I was posted to the Far East and during the trouble we were required to keep up a fighter umbrella. This means I had to decide which aircraft to service first and which had to be left to the last. Imagine a line of fighters as one taxies to the far end and one to the other. We were short staffed in my trade. I trusted God to guide me to the right plane and in my mind came a quiet voice. I obeyed the code letters and raced to that aircraft. As I did, my heart was filled with joy to the brim. After the trouble was over I worked it out to 360 aircraft checked without the mistake of servicing the wrong one. I can write a small book about how God has guided me and also fill it with everyday happenings which I know come from our Maker, not the subconscious.[13]

It seems obvious to me that his long experience enabled him to know which planes to service first; or at least if he was mistaken his 'divine revelation' would nevertheless have assured him that he was right! And we have all come across people who are convinced that God told them to do something when it seems clear that this was either simply what they themselves wanted to do or what their common sense told them to do. Again, there have been insane people who committed murder in obedience to what they took to be a divine command. So I grant fully that there is plenty of scope for self-delusion in hearing voices and seeing visions. But this is something of which the great mystics themselves were well aware. In the medieval world they generally thought of what we call self-delusion as being deceived by the devil. For them the test – apart from the test of doctrinal orthodoxy – was the long-term effect in the person's life. For example, St Teresa of Avila was acutely conscious of this danger but was persuaded of the genuineness of her own visions by their fruits in her life, which were evident to everyone. She uses the analogy of someone who encounters a stranger who leaves her a gift of jewels. If some one else later suggested that the stranger had been a mere apparition, the jewels left in her hand would prove otherwise. And, in the case of her visions,

> I could show [any doubters] these jewels – for all who knew me were well aware how my soul had changed: my confessor himself testified to this, for the difference was very great in every respect, and no fancy, but such as all could clearly see. And as I had previously been so wicked, I concluded, I could not believe that, if the devil were doing this to delude me and drag me down to hell, he would make use of means which so completely defeated their own ends by taking away my vices and making me virtuous and strong; for it was quite clear to me that these experiences had immediately made me a different person.[14]

And in general, among the mystics of each tradition, the difference between delusion and reality is shown by the presence or absence of a long-term transforming effect in the individual's personality and life.

DAVID: Right. But delusions and false beliefs can also have good effects. Think of the effect of placebos in medicine. And if, as I believe, there is no transcendent Reality, the sincere conviction that there is may nevertheless make people happier and more charitable towards others. Indeed there's evidence that this is so. Religion may well sometimes be a useful delusion, though of course also sometimes a very dangerous delusion. But either way it is a delusion.

JOHN: Yes, agreed. But let me explain why I think that those who do participate in the realm of religious experience are entitled to trust it.

DAVID: Alright, go ahead.

6
Trusting Religious Experience

DAVID: So I presume that you're arguing from religious experience to God, or the supranatural, as its cause?

JOHN: No, definitely not that. It's the quite different argument that those who participate in the realm of religious experience are, as rational people, fully entitled to trust it.

DAVID: But not those of us who do not experience religiously?

JOHN: It's not quite as simple as that, because there are in fact many people whose own religious experience is too slight or weak or even non-existent to make them believe in a transcendent reality, but who do nevertheless believe, or sometimes believe, because of the experience witnessed to by the great religious figures – or that plus someone they know personally who is sufficiently spiritually impressive to reinforce that witness.

DAVID: So they're parasitic on what you call the great figures, such as Jesus, for example, or the Buddha?

JOHN: Yes, exactly.

DAVID: Okay. So let's leave those people aside and concentrate on those who do, as you put it, participate in the realm of religious experience, and sufficiently so to make them believe in a transcendent reality of some kind. You are claiming that it is rational for them to believe this. I'm not of course saying, against this, that all religious believers are irrational; but I do say that they are deluding themselves. So what do you reckon justifies rational people in being religious? After all, as Richard Dawkins says, the existence of God is 'a scientific hypothesis like any other'.[1]

JOHN: No, it's not a scientific hypothesis. That's his most fundamental error. There are two reasons why it is not a scientific hypothesis. One is that, as my friend Keith Ward has pointed out, a scientific theory or hypothesis involves observations that are in principle repeatable and give rise to predictions that can be confirmed or disconfirmed. So Keith Ward concludes that the existence of God 'is a philosophical or metaphysical hypothesis'.[2] I agree with him that the existence of God is not a scientific hypothesis, but I want to go further. It's not a hypothesis at all. It is in the same category as other fundamental beliefs which are not based on inference from evidence but on direct experience.

DAVID: Such as?

JOHN: Well to start with, we are directly aware of the content of our present visual field. We don't infer it – there is nothing to infer it from – and we can't offer any evidence for it. The only evidence is itself. In other words, it doesn't need any evidence and isn't capable of any.

DAVID: True, but what beyond that?

JOHN: The belief that there is an external world in which we interact with other people. We don't infer the surrounding world, we experience it. We see it, hear it, touch it, taste it, smell it. But we can't prove that it exists outside our own consciousness.

DAVID: But in this case there's no alternative to the reality of the perceived world. We cannot suppose that there is no external world, whereas there is an alternative to the reality of a transcendent reality, namely, that there is no such reality.

JOHN: But there is an alternative to there being an external world – solipsism, the theory that only I exist and the world and other people exist only in my consciousness, like a dream environment including the people in it, all of which exist only while I am dreaming.

DAVID: But surely no one has seriously believed that?

JOHN: George Berkeley,[3] who was one of the great British philosophers, argued for what he called immaterialism, the idea that *to be is to be perceived*. The world exists only in our consciousness. And he only saved himself from solipsism by invoking God as the immediate cause of all our experiences, coordinating the perceptions of different people so that we interact with other perceivers in what appears to be a common environment.

DAVID: He was, wasn't he, a religious believer – indeed an Anglican bishop – which enabled him to stop short of solipsism. But to invoke God at this point is to bring in theology to save your philosophy – something that you can't expect everyone to accept.

JOHN: Yes, I agree. And of course another problem with solipsism is that it can only be stated in the first person, in spite of the lady who once wrote to Bertrand Russell to say that she was a solipsist and was surprised that no one else seemed to believe in it![4] But whether or not there are people who believe it, it is a theory that cannot be refuted. So David Hume made the right next move after Berkeley when he argued that belief in the external world cannot be either proved or disproved but is what can be called a natural belief. He said,

> Nature has not left this to [our] choice, and has doubtless esteem'd it an affair of too great importance to be trusted to our uncertain reasonings and speculations. We may well ask, What causes induce us to believe in the existence of body [i.e. a material world]? But 'tis vain to ask, Whether there be body or not? That is a point, which we must take for granted in all our reasonings.[5]

And the reason why we have to take its reality for granted is simply that the world impresses itself upon us. We can't help being conscious of it.

DAVID: Okay. But what has this to do with religion?

JOHN: The next step is from sense experience to religious experience, the bridge between them being the universally accepted principle of critical trust. This is the basic principle by which we all live every day: we trust our experience, except when we have – or think we have – good reason not to. If something seems to be there, then it is rational to take it that it is indeed there unless, as I said, we have reason to doubt the experience. Surely this is part of our working definition of rationality, or even of sanity. It would be irrational to experience, visually, a brick wall in front of you and walk straight into it as though it wasn't there. That would only be rational if you knew that it was a hologram and not a real wall. Knowing it to be a hologram would be a good reason not to take the experience at face value. But, in the absence of any reason to distrust our experience, it is always rational to trust it – this is the principle of critical trust.

DAVID: Yes, that's okay. I can accept that general principle. But in the case of religious experience we do have good reasons to distrust it.

JOHN: Namely?

DAVID: Well, first of all, as you said yourself, our sense experience forces itself upon us. We can't not be aware of the physical world because it impinges on our senses all the time. Our awareness of it is compulsory. But no supranatural environment impresses itself compulsorily upon us. Isn't this a good reason for doubting religious experience, a decisive reason for those of us who have never ourselves experienced religiously, and at least a very troubling fact for those of you who have?

That's one reason for distrusting religious experience, and another follows from it. Because sense experience is compulsory, it's universal. It applies impartially to everyone, throughout the world. You said that in the UK and USA about a third of people report some kind of special experience at least once. It may be that the visions and auditions of some of the famous mystics were coercive to them, as hallucinations can be, but surely not the relatively unspectacular kind you were

citing? And that's very different from everyone everywhere always experiencing our material environment.

And then a third reason is that whereas sense experience is uniform around the world religious experience
is not. We all experience the same natural environment,
but there are many different and rival perceptions
of the alleged supranatural environment. Some say
that it is a personal God, and among these some say
that it is the Adonai, the Lord, of rabbinic Judaism;
some that it is the Holy Trinity of Christianity; some
that it is the Allah of Islam; and yet others that it is the
Vishnu or Shiva of theistic Hinduism. But others again
say that the supranatural reality is not a personal God
at all but the transpersonal Brahman or Dharmakaya
or Tao. All of which suggests that we are dealing with
culturally varying figments of the human imagination.

So here are three interlinked reasons, and I reckon
very good reasons, for trusting sense experience and
distrusting religious experience.

JOHN: Yes, and all at first sight valid points. But I suggest
to you that these three differences – compulsory/not
compulsory, universal/not universal, and uniform/
not uniform – are all appropriate to the very different
natures of the supposed realities being experienced.

DAVID: How's that?

JOHN: First, the physical world *has* to force itself on
our attention if we are to survive within it as the vul-
nerable organisms that we are. But this compulsory
awareness does not undermine our personal and moral
freedom. It sets the scene, and the limits, within which
we exercise that freedom. This is because the material
world in itself is value-free – it's just the brute fact to

which we have continually to adapt ourselves. But suppose, as the religions claim, that we are living at the same time within a supranatural environment which is not value-free but is such that our awareness of it has to be unforced if we are to exist within it as persons – in other words, as free moral and spiritual beings.

DAVID: But if there is that supranatural environment as well as our natural environment, why should it not present itself to us equally compellingly? If we need to be aware of it for our own good, why should it hide from us?

JOHN: It's easiest to make the point in theistic terms. If we were automatically confronted, whether we wanted to be or not, by a Being of infinite goodness and love, infinite power, infinite knowledge, we would not be free and responsible creatures in relation to that Being. His or her knowledge would see into every corner of our inner being, all our thoughts and feelings and imaginings being transparent all the time to the divine gaze. Infinite power would totally overshadow us, and infinite goodness and love would by its very presence make a total and irresistible claim on us. We would be physically free, but we would not be intellectually free to believe in God because there would be no alternative. And we would not be morally and spiritually free because there would be no genuine alternative to responding in obedience and worship to such a Being. So in order for us to exist as finite, free creatures in the presence of God, he or she must set us at a distance from Godself – not a spatial distance but a distance in the dimension of knowledge, in philosophical language an epistemic distance. Or, putting it in the way I put it before, we have to find ourselves in an ambiguous universe – in fact the kind of universe we do in fact find ourselves in. And yet at the same time there is an aspect of our nature that naturally tends to experience the natural in terms of the supranatural – although within the naturalistic assumption of our modern Western culture it is easy to suppress that tendency.

DAVID: I think I can see the point about what you call epistemic distance. Also about a religious tendency – because some kind of religion seems to go back as early as we can trace human life. But are you going to say, with many preachers of the past, and a few fundamentalists today, that it is sin that makes us suppress that tendency?

JOHN: No, though a self-concern that blinds us to challenging realities is something that affects all of us, believers and non-believers alike. But the main barrier is intellectual. In atheist societies – Stalinist Russia, Mao's China – people were brought up to think of religion as illusion. But, more importantly for us in our society, the pervasive naturalistic assumption – which, I've argued, is only an assumption – functions to suppress the religious side of our nature. People think in terms of a false contrast between science and fantasy.

DAVID: I hear what you're saying there, though I don't accept it for a moment. But just to complete it, you spelled out the idea of epistemic distance in theistic terms, but what about the non-theistic religions, the religions in which the Ultimate is not thought of as a divine Person but as a reality transcending the personal/impersonal distinction – particularly Buddhism?

JOHN: Right. The same principle of distance between ourselves and ultimate reality applies, though in a different way. In Buddhism, instead of an infinite Person whose direct presence would be overwhelming, there is a nirvanic state which cannot be known and experienced by us except through a long process of ego transcendence. This process was spelled out by the Buddha as the Noble Eightfold Path, which is partly the practice of meditation, partly a matter of spiritual understanding, partly of ethical living – telling the truth and avoiding harmful gossip or slander; non-violence; not earning your living in ways destructive of the human community, such as dealing in armaments or harmful drugs – and more comprehensively by developing the basic virtues of *karuna* or compassion, feeling with and for others, and *metta* or loving kindness. As the ego point of view, in which we experience everything primarily as it affects ourself, is gradually overcome, the 'distance' from the goal reduces. I suppose we could say that the distance is not purely epistemic, in the dimension of knowledge, but primarily spiritual, leading to direct knowledge. And the spiritual distance involves an epistemic distance.

DAVID: Okay. I don't profess to know much about Buddhism, and I'll have to take your word for that. But there's still an important bit of unfinished business, namely, if religious experience is a human awareness of the Transcendent, how is it that that awareness takes such different forms – in contrast to sense experience?

JOHN: That's a good question. Let's make that the next item on the agenda.

7
Despite the Religious Contradictions?

JOHN: Yes, what about the numerous contradictions between the different religions? I have to begin with epistemology, the question of how we know anything and what are the limits of knowledge.

DAVID: Okay, go ahead.

JOHN: Well, to start with sense perception, the belief that there is an external world is called realism. And we then have to distinguish between naive realism and critical realism. Naive realism assumes that the world is just as we perceive it. But of course it isn't. We see things as they are for us, with our particular sensory and cognitive equipment, not as they are in themselves, unperceived. Different animals perceive the world differently. The senses are selective in that they are only attuned to those limited aspects of our total environment that are relevant to us as living organisms adapted to surviving within it. For example, out of the electro-magnetic spectrum from cosmic rays as short as four ten-thousand-millionths of an inch to radio waves as long as eighteen miles, we only pick up those between sixteen and thirty-two millionths of an inch. We only hear a certain range of sounds, while some other animals, such as dogs and horses, can hear sounds much higher than we do. Each species detects that selection from the whole that it needs to be aware of within its particular biological niche. To be aware of more than this would only confuse and distract us. For example, if we saw this table, not as a brown-coloured solid object on which we can put our cups of coffee, but as mostly empty space with millions of minute particles moving about at an immense speed, we would be completely bewildered.

In our case, we rely – apart of course from those who are blind – mainly on sight. But elephants have poor eyesight and rely more on sound and smell, which are both very acute. It is said that they can even hear through their feet, which are sensitive to vibrations in the earth. In contrast, bats rely for identifying nearby objects on a sonar echo system. The world in which elephants live must be very different from the bats' world, and both very different from our world. But critical realism takes account of all this. It acknowledges that we are conscious of the world as it appears to us, not as it is in itself, and it acknowledges at the same time that there can be a range of different perceptions of the same environment.

The mind then gets to work interpreting, by means of concepts, what the senses present to it. We can approach this through ambiguous pictures. It was Wittgenstein who first drew attention to this. For example, the goblet that can also be seen as two faces gazing at each other, or the one that he used in his *Philosophical Investigations*,[1] the duck-rabbit. You can see it as the outline of a duck facing left or of a rabbit facing right, and usually the mind switches back and forth between them. So he introduced the term seeing-as. Wittgenstein thought that this applied only to ambiguous figures, however, and not to ordinary objects, such as a knife and fork. As he pointed out, we do not see them *as* a knife and fork because, he thought, there is no ambiguity in such cases. However, I believe he was mistaken at this point. It is true that you and I can only see the knife and fork the way we do. But if you could bring a stone-age person here in a time-machine they would not see what is on the table as a knife and fork, because they would not have these concepts or their other surrounding cultural concepts, such as table, chair, sitting at table and eating a meal off a plate, and so on. They might see them as small weapons, or as sacred objects full of *mana,* or in some other way. So even in ordinary life we are seeing things *as* in a particular way. In fact, all seeing is seeing-as. And we can expand seeing-as into experiencing-as by including not only sight but all the senses as well – and we are in fact nearly always using more than one at a time.

DAVID: Yes, critical realism sounds right. But what has this to do with religious belief?

JOHN: Well the next step is to say that religious belief is not properly based either on philosophical arguments, as we've agreed, or, as I think you'll also agree, on any human authority such as the Church, but in my view on religious experience.

DAVID: Yes, that's your view of religion, and I can go along with it for the sake of argument.

JOHN: Okay. Now, it seems clear, to take an obvious case, that Jesus was intensely conscious of living in the presence of his heavenly Father. He did not see God with his eyes, but he was so powerfully aware of God that God was as real to him as were his companions or the hills and lake of Galilee. Now I claim that it was rational for him to believe in the reality of God and, not only that, it would have been irrational for him not to. It would have been a kind of cognitive suicide.

Again, Muhammad was intensely conscious of the divine presence, through the words impressed upon him that became the Qur'an. And again, it would have been a kind of cognitive suicide for him not to accept these words as a divine revelation.

Yet again, the Buddha when he attained to enlightenment, or liberation from the ego point of view, and enjoyed the supreme bliss of nirvana, could not help being aware of this reality, indeed of participating in it. It would have been unthinkable not to, again a kind of cognitive suicide.

DAVID: Well yes, no doubt. But that doesn't show that they were right. They may have been deluded. Delusions can be overwhelmingly powerful. And indeed they can't all have been right because what they each believed they were conscious of was so different. As you were saying yourself earlier, the heavenly Father of Jesus was not the same as the Allah of the Qur'an, and neither was at all like the nirvana of the Buddha. Doesn't that show that out of three at least two must have been deluded, and most likely all three?

JOHN: It would if we were naive realists believing that we are aware of things as they are in themselves. But not if we are critical realists. We can then see the direct objects of these three very different experiences as appearances to different mentalities of the same reality. If you live within a theistic culture, as both Jesus and Muhammad did, taking it for granted that the Ultimate is a personal God, then your religious experience will take a theistic form. And the practice of prayer will reinforce this. But if you live in the Hindu culture of the Buddha's India, believing in an ultimate reality beyond the god figures, and you are practising meditation rather than I–Thou prayer, you will encounter the Ultimate, the same Ultimate, in a quite different way.

DAVID: The same reality experienced in different ways! I agree that this happens in sense perception, but is there any reason to think that that can happen in the case of religion?

JOHN: Yes, there's even some experimental evidence. Two American neuro-scientists, Eugene d'Aquili and Andrew Newberg, conducted experiments with a group of Tibeten Buddhist meditators and a group of Franciscan nuns. Using SPECT – single photon emission computed tomography – to record the blood flow, and hence the oxygen flow, in their subjects' brains when at the high point of their meditation, they found exactly the same neural changes in both groups. But the results of this in consciousness were strikingly different in the two groups. The Buddhists reported a sense of oneness with the universe and of peace and happiness, while the Christian nuns reported a sense of the closeness of God and a mingling with him.[2] Why this difference? Clearly it must be due to their different conceptual systems. The Catholic nuns believed in a personal God, while the Buddhist monks believed in an ultimate reality beyond the distinction between the personal and the impersonal. The same receptivity to something beyond them came to consciousness in the two groups in accordance with their different conceptual systems.

DAVID: Okay. As a very general theory I can see that as something worth exploring further. Let's do that before returning to the main argument. Do you find the idea of experiencing-as, with the possibility of the mind switching from one interpretation to another as in Wittgenstein's duck-rabbit kind of case, in the religions themselves?

JOHN: The only one with an explicit doctrine like this is the strand in Buddhism which teaches that *samsara*, the world of *dukkha*, transitoriness and suffering, is identical with *nirvana*, the ultimately desirable but indescribable state. So samsara and nirvana are the same world experienced in radically different ways, one from an ego-centred point of view and the other in a way that has transcended ego concerns. To quote D. T. Suzuki, who was the leading exponent of Zen Buddhism in the West,

> Our entire surroundings are viewed from quite an unexpected angle of perception. Whatever this is, the world for those who have gained a satori [the moment of enlightenment] is no more the old world as it used to be;

even with all its flowing streams and burning fires, it is never the same again ... This is a mystery and a miracle, but according to the Zen masters such is being performed every day.[3]

But in the theistic traditions we can also see many examples of religious experiencing-as. The Hebrew prophet Jeremiah seems to have experienced the invading Chaldean army as God's instrument to punish the erring Israelites. As he expressed it in his preaching, this was not so much an intellectual judgement as the way he actually experienced the events at the time. And within Christianity, to pick out a couple of examples, the American evangelist Jonathan Edwards told how 'the appearance of everything was altered; there seems to be, as it were, a calm, sweet cast, or appearance of divine glory, in almost everything',[4] and George Fox, the founder of the Quaker movement, told how 'All things were new; and all the creation gave another smell unto me than before, beyond what words can utter ... '[5] And there are innumerable other examples. We saw that when we were looking at religious experience. In fact the more experiential strand of the religions is a form of religious experiencing-as.

DAVID: Interesting. Does this connect at all with modern philosophy?

JOHN: Yes, and with even wider implications which take us back to our original question about the different and contradictory forms that religion takes. It's Kant's distinction between the noumenal and the phenomenal, but applied, as Kant himself did not, to religion. The Ultimate is the unexperiencable noumenal reality which is humanly thought and experienced in terms of different human conceptualities as the phenomenal Gods and trans-personal Absolutes of the world religions. Human religious experience is schematized, to continue to use Kantian language, not in terms of abstract time, as in Kant's system, but in terms of the filled time of history and culture. The concept of personality gives rise to the theisms, and the concept of the absolute gives rise to the non-theistic traditions. But while this is indeed an application of Kant's distinction, the basic idea goes back long before Kant to the brilliant statement of Thomas Aquinas, 'Things known are in the knower according to the mode of the knower.'[6] Of course Aquinas did not apply this to the plurality of religions, but in fact 'the mode of the knower' differs between the different ways of being human that are the great cultures of the earth, within which the different religious traditions have grown up. So I want to say that the Ultimate, as the 'thing known', is in the human knower in a variety of different ways – as the Adonai of Judaism, the Heavenly Father of Christianity and the Allah of Islam, and also as the foci of meditation and enlightenment within the non-theistic faiths.

DAVID: There are several things here that need a lot more explanation if they are to make sense to me. First, are you saying that what you call the Ultimate, ultimate reality, is unknowable?

JOHN: Yes, unknowable to us as it is in itself. But knowable by us in its impact upon us, which takes various forms in religious experience. Although a radical thought in the West, it has been familiar in India for many centuries. For example, Kabir (fifteenth century CE) said that 'The formless God takes a thousand forms in the eyes of His creatures.'[7]

DAVID: Yes, I think I see what you're after. But surely this is a complete departure from what all of the religions themselves teach, and can never be acceptable to any of them. A monotheist – Jewish, Christian or Muslim – could never agree that what they experience as the presence of God is being experienced by Buddhists non-theistically.

JOHN: Yes and No. It's not acceptable to the leaders of the religious organizations. But it is nevertheless present in the mystical strand within each of the great traditions. I can approach this, as a Christian, through the Christian mystics. Some of them, such as Meister Eckhart, distinguish between the Godhead, the ultimate reality, which is ineffable, or as I would rather say transcategorial, beyond the scope of our human categories of thought, and the God of the Bible and of Christian worship. As Eckhart said, 'God and the Godhead are as different from each other as heaven and earth',[8] for 'God acts. The Godhead does not.'[9] We find a parallel distinction in Hinduism in the distinction between *nirguna* – without attributes – Brahman, which is the ultimate reality in itself, beyond all human thought forms, and *saguna* – with attributes – Brahman, which is that same reality as humanly thought and experienced as Ishwara, God, and the realm of the worshipped deities. Again, in Mahayana Buddhism the distinction is between the Dharmakaya, the ultimate transcategorial reality, and the realm of the heavenly Buddhas, one or other of whom becomes incarnate on earth from time to time. And in Jewish (Kabbala) mysticism the distinction is between *En Sof*, 'the Infinite', and the worshipped God of the scriptures. As Gershom Scholem explains, Jewish mystics affirm both 'the hidden God who remains eternally unknowable in the depths of His own self, or, to use the bold expression of the Kabbalists "in the depth of His nothingness"', 'without special attributes', and 'the living presence of God, the god of the Bible, who is good, wise, just and merciful'. So they affirm both 'the hidden God of whom nothing is known to us, and the living God of religious experience and revelation', the latter being the former as humanly encountered.[10] And in the Sufi mysticism of Islam the distinction is between *al Haqq*, 'the Real', the ineffable Ultimate Reality, and the revealed Allah of the Qur'an. Thus Ibn al-'Arabi said, 'The Essence, as being beyond all these relationships, is not a divinity ... it is we who make Him a divinity by being that through which He knows himself as Divine. Thus he is not known [as God] until we are known.'[11] In each case, the transcategorial Real, beyond the scope of our human conceptualities, and its humanly knowable forms are not two different realities but the same reality as it is in itself and in the ways in which it impacts our human consciousness. And the mystics are people who feel the presence of the Transcendent although they do not see it – like the wind, you feel it but do not see it.

DAVID: Okay, so the more mystical side of religion uses this distinction. But what about the non-mystical majority? Would the Pope or the Archbishop of Canterbury or the Presbyterians, Baptists, Methodists and so on accept it? Or the Ayatollahs, Muftis, Rabbis and so on? Surely they would all see it as undermining the distinctive claim of their own tradition to be the supreme truth.

JOHN: Yes, that's true; although the great Catholic theologian Karl Rahner once said that 'In the future Christians will be mystics, or they will not be anything.'[12] But nevertheless most church leaders do reject what is called religious pluralism; but so what?

DAVID: So what, as you say. But in order to meet the major problem I raised about the religions all contradicting one another, so that we can dismiss them all, you will have to add, won't you, that the different supposed awarenesses of the divine noumenon are *equally authentic*? Otherwise one of them could be authentic while all the others could be dismissed. But since they all claim to be the one-and-only authentic religion, you would be back in the situation of the impartial observer having to dismiss them all.

JOHN: Yes, that's right. There has to be a criterion of authenticity, and there is, and it's drawn from the religions themselves. Its essence is 'By their fruits you shall know them.' It consists in a re-centring in the Ultimate which shows itself in a personal transformation from self-concern, or selfishness, to a concern for others. To sample from West to East: for the Christian, this recentring is expressed practically in loving your neighbour as you love yourself. The criterion is again practical for the Muslim:

> Piety does not lie in turning your face to East or West: piety lies in believing in God, the Last Day and the

angels, the Scriptures and the prophets, and disburs-
ing your wealth out of love of God among your kin and
the orphans, the wayfarers and mendicants, freeing the
slaves, observing your devotional obligations, and in
paying the zakat (alms) and fulfilling a pledge you have
given, and being patient in hardship, adversity, and
times of peril.[13]

Moving to the East, within Buddhism the sign that
someone is on the way to liberation or enlightenment
is that they are becoming free from 'malevolence,
anger, malice, hypocrisy, spite, envy, stinginess, deceit,
treachery, impetuosity, pride, conceit, indolence'.[14]
And I suggest that all of the major world religions are,
so far as we can tell, more or less equally successful –
and of course also equally unsuccessful – as contexts
of the salvific transformation of human existence
from natural self-centeredness to a new orientation
centred in the Transcendent.

DAVID: You can claim that, but can you substantiate it?

JOHN: I can't prove it, certainly. But take first personal
transformation. There are good and bad, saints and
sinners, within all religious communities. We don't
have any statistics to help us, any register of saints.
But when you look around the world, and particularly
when you travel in the heartlands of the different religions and get to know people of those faiths, I think
most people would agree that, so far as we can tell,
saints and sinners seem to be sprinkled pretty evenly
among them.

DAVID: But what do you mean by a saint? I gather that
the last Pope, John Paul II, created 482 saints, more

than all his predecessors put together during the last five hundred years. Are these examples of what you mean?

JOHN: No, though I'm sure some of them were, and equally sure that some were not but were declared saints for political, including ecclesiastical political, reasons. I mean by a saint – or a mahatma, a great soul – a man or a woman who is living out to an exceptional degree the universally recognized virtues of human goodness, love and concern and self-giving for others in need. I also want to include more contemplative people who are manifestly much closer to God or to the Transcendent than the rest of us, and whose wisdom and faith inspire others. But there has been a very significant historical change in comparatively recent times. Centuries ago saintly people generally had no political power or opportunity to influence the structures of society. They often lived in monasteries and nunneries, influencing the world only by prayer and individual charity. But within the last hundred and fifty or so years we have seen the new phenomenon of the political saint. I suppose the greatest example so far has been Mahatma Gandhi, and there have been Vinoba Bhave, also in India, and more recently Martin Luther King in the United States, archbishop Oscar Romero in San Salvador and archbishop Helder Camera in Brazil,[15] and Dag Hommarskjold of Sweden and the United Nations, and today Nelson Mandela and Desmond Tutu in South Africa, and Thich Nat Hahn in Thailand – and innumerable less well-known figures in every country. But of course a saint is not a perfect human being – there have never been any such. Saintliness is a matter of degree, not simply of ticking a Yes or No box.

DAVID: And no doubt also a number of purely secular 'saints', likewise in varying degrees.

JOHN: Yes indeed. And it's worth emphasizing that saintliness doesn't depend upon what someone believes but on how they live. So today, in our increasingly secular West, there are more secular saints, in their varying degrees, than ever before. People can and do feel the claim of the Transcendent on their lives in purely moral terms without using any religious concepts – and without being aware that they are responding to the Transcendent. But let me now put this into a wider context, by bringing in the idea of meaning.

DAVID: But I understand that there are many meanings of 'meaning'. What do *you* mean by it?

JOHN: Meaning in the sense I'm using the term is always meaning *for* someone, or for a group of people. In the case of a thing, an object, its meaning for us consists in the way we think it appropriate to behave in relation to it. So the meaning for us of a knife and fork is that we use them as tools for eating. But most of the time we are living in relation not to isolated objects but to situations of which we are a part. A situation consists of many objects but has a meaning beyond that of the sum of its constituent parts. And its meaning for us is the way we think it appropriate to behave within it. Our present situation is one of talking together about some fairly basic philosophical problems; and we behave within this situation by continuing to do what we are doing. Okay?

DAVID: Yes, that's okay so far.

JOHN: The next step is to notice that there can be levels of meaning in situations. At one level there is purely physical meaning. But superimposed on this there may be a moral or social meaning.

DAVID: You're equating social and moral?

JOHN: Yes, the moral meaning of a situation always arises from the fact that it involves other people.

DAVID: Okay.

JOHN: So let's suppose there is a car accident and someone is hurt and bleeding. The physical meaning is just the fact of the road, the metal cars, the physical body in the seat of one of the cars, the blood streaming from the head. But simultaneously, on another level, there is the ethical situation of someone in urgent need of help and a moral obligation on anyone who can help to do so. If they have the necessary skill they may have an obligation to apply first aid, and ask someone else to ring for an ambulance. Or, if they can't do this, just to ring for an ambulance. Or, of course, someone may already have done all that. But when it's up to us to do something, I think we all feel an obligation to do so. And this ethical meaning of the situation is superimposed on its purely physical meaning. It's a higher level of meaning in the same situation.

DAVID: Higher?

JOHN: In the sense that moral presupposes physical meaning. There has to be a physical situation for it to have any moral meaning.

DAVID: But what about those individuals, fortunately rather rare, who seem to have no moral sense at all?

There are occasionally people who commit horrible crimes, murder and torture, but feel no remorse at all.

JOHN: Yes, I'm afraid there are. And I don't know what the reason is. Is it due to upbringing and life circumstances, or is it due to some neural malfunction, or what? I don't know. Do you?

DAVID: No, I don't know either. I expect there are various theories, but it's not something that I've looked into.

JOHN: Well, moving on, there is also aesthetic meaning, the artistic nature of a painting, or sculpture, or a piece of music, or a poem, or indeed the natural world. Here again there is some physical material that carries a more than purely physical meaning. This applies more to objects than to situations. But rather than elaborate on that, I'd like to move on to yet another level of meaning, the religious meaning of situations.

DAVID: If there is such a thing.

JOHN: I said that meaning is always meaning *for* someone. And for those who participate in the realm of religious experience, situations can have not only a physical, and usually also a moral, but also a religious meaning. They experience situations and events as mediating a divine presence or a universal transcendence. This can be individual or communal. When we were discussing religious experience I quoted a few examples of reported experiences in which the whole environment takes on a new meaning of rightness so that there can be nothing to fear or worry about. These were individual experiences. For most of us such experiences are very occasional and vary in degree of intensity from very slight to very powerful. But for the great saints and mahatmas they are more pervasive and continuous and extremely powerful. And communally, sometimes in a church service, for example, there is a sacramental experience of divine presence. Indeed in the earliest days of humanity religious experience seems to have been communal rather than individual.

DAVID: Always supposing that there is some kind of transcendent reality to be experienced, which of course I don't believe there is.

JOHN: Yes I know. The religious ambiguity of the universe still remains intact.

DAVID: Actually, I'm not sure it does. Because there's another reason of a different kind altogether for distrusting religious experience.

JOHN: Is there? We'd better look at it.

8
Neuroscience and Religious Experience

JOHN: Okay, go ahead.

DAVID: This reason for not trusting religious experience is comparatively new, in the sense that it has come to light in the twentieth and twenty-first centuries. It comes from work in the neurosciences, which I know is something that you also have long been interested in. Some experimenters claim to have located an area in the temporal lobe which produces intense feelings of spiritual transcendence combined with a sense of a mystical presence. A Canadian researcher reports that, by stimulating this area,

> Typically people report a presence. One time we had a strobe light going and this individual actually saw Christ in the strobe. [Another] experienced God visiting her. Afterwards we looked at her EEG and there was this classic spike and slow-wave seizure over the temporal lobe at the precise time of the experience.[1]

So stimulating certain areas of the temporal lobe can produce a sense of divine presence. The same researcher,

Michael Persinger, developed a helmet to do this, and Rita Carter says that 'nearly all who have used it report the sensation of a presence. Many also see religious visions such as the Virgin Mary or Jesus.'[2]

Again, as the neurophysiologist V. S. Ramachandran says, 'Every medical student is taught that patients with epileptic seizures originating in [the left temporal lobe] can have intense, spiritual experiences during the seizures and sometimes become preoccupied with religious and moral issues even during the seizure-free or interictal periods.'[3] In other words, a purely physical cause can produce religious experiences. And this is because a particular episode of conscious thinking and the particular electro-chemical processes taking place in the brain at the same time are not two distinct processes, one physical and the other not, but they're one-and-the same physical event.

JOHN: Yes, I know that that's the accepted naturalistic view. But it faces formidable difficulties. The basic problem that I see is the fundamental difference between physical and mental states. Suppose a neurosurgeon has exposed a patient's brain, perhaps in order to find the seat of her epileptic seizures, and with instruments registering its electrical activity is tracing the successive coordinated firings of the neurons correlated with the patient's reports of what is going on in her consciousness. Because the brain has no pain nerves the patient can be conscious during the operation, and indeed as you know this can sometimes be very helpful to the surgeon. Suppose, for example, she's visualizing a vivid red sunset on the horizon of an ocean of grey-green water, with a ship passing from right to left in the middle distance.

Does it really make sense to say that the electro-chemical activity that the surgeon is monitoring with his instruments, taking place in the grey matter that he can see in front of him and touch, literally *is* that visualized sunset scene which forms the content of the patient's consciousness? Mental states are not located at some point in space, whereas brain states are; the conscious sensation of pain, for example, can be sharp or dull or throbbing, but no part of the brain itself goes dull or becomes sharp or starts throbbing. It makes sense to say that the brain activity *causes* the conscious experience. It makes sense to say that there could be no conscious experience without that brain activity. But does it make sense to say that the brain activity literally is, identically, the visualized scene occupying the patient's consciousness? To me, that is counter-intuitive to the point of being actually unintelligible. I know that this appeal to ordinary experience is dismissed by some neuroscientists as folk-psychology. But that's pejorative spin language. While there is an immense body of evidence for full consciousness/brain correlation, to suppose that any accumulation of this evidence, however great, constitutes evidence for their identity is simply an elementary fallacy.

DAVID: But there are plenty of examples of phenomena that can be described in different ways, in the language of different disciplines, while being the same thing. For example, you can describe a flash of lightning as the seen sudden thin zigzag of bright light in the sky and also, if you are a physicist, as the massive sudden discharge of the collective electricity generated by the movement of many slightly charged water droplets or ice crystals that form the clouds. So in spite of the fact that they are described quite differently they are in actual fact the same thing.

JOHN: Yes, that's true. But does it help to make brain/consciousness identity plausible? When you take examples of two things which are both uncontroversially physical, like a flash of lightning and a cloud-generated electrical discharge, you're begging the question – which is not whether two physical phenomena can be identical but whether a physical phenomenon can be identical with a *mental* phenomenon. Instead of taking the electrical discharge as the second term of the analogy you should take the conscious seeing of the flash. The question is whether that conscious episode is itself something physical. And the fact that the electrical discharge and the flash of light are the same does nothing to show that our consciousness of the flash is physical.

DAVID: Okay. Let's take the consciousness of the flash. This can be described on one level as neuron firings, and on another level as the conscious sensation of seeing a flash, so that the neuron firings and the conscious experience are the same thing described in different terms for different purposes.

JOHN: You're begging the question again. The question is how a conscious experience can be identical with a physical event in the brain, as distinguished from being precisely correlated with it. I say that it doesn't even make sense to say that they are literally identical.

DAVID: Well, most people working in the neurosciences today do take their identity for granted.

JOHN: Yes, they do. Because they nearly all take for granted the naturalistic assumption of our culture. But for the most part they are working on some very specific small area of the brain and are not interested in what they call the philosophical questions. However, those leading figures who do take an interest in the larger questions have concluded that consciousness is a sheer mystery. And if it's a sheer mystery they can't know that it is identical with brain activity.

DAVID: Who do you have in mind?

JOHN: Well, V. S. Ramachandran of the Center for Brain and Cognition at the University of California, San Diego, whom you quoted earlier, says that 'despite two hundred years of research, the most basic questions about the human mind ... remain unanswered, as does the really big question: What is consciousness?'[4] Roger Penrose of Oxford says that 'conscious actions and conscious perceptions – and, in particular, the conscious phenomenon of understanding – will find no proper explanation within the present-day picture of the material universe'.[5] And Steven Rose of the Brain and Behaviour Group at the Open University, UK, says that 'the issue of consciousness lies beyond mere neuroscience'.[6] And another distinguished researcher, Benjamin Libet of the University of California at Los Angeles, says that 'There is an unexplained gap between the category of physical phenomena and the category of subjective phenomena ... The assumption that a deterministic nature of the physically observable world (to the extent that it may be true) can account for subjective conscious functions and events is a *belief,* not a scientifically proven proposition.'[7]

DAVID: But it's still true, is it not, that they nearly all assume that even if we don't understand how this is so, yet nevertheless somehow the mind is simply the brain at work?

JOHN: Yes, they do assume that. But it *is* an assumption. It's not a genuine scientific hypothesis.

DAVID: Not a scientific hypothesis?

JOHN: No. I take it you accept, as most of us do today, Karl Popper's doctrine that while a large-scale scientific hypothesis can never be absolutely verified if true, but only shown to have a certain degree of probability, it can, at least in principle, be decisively falsified if false, and that this is an essential feature of any genuine scientific hypothesis. If there is no possible observation or experiment that could ever decisively contradict it, it's not a scientific hypothesis. That a flash of lighting is an electric discharge could be experimentally falsified, if it were in fact false, by finding that there is no electrical activity taking place. But there is no way in which the identity of an electrochemical event and a moment of consciousness could be empirically falsified if false. The identity thesis reflects a presupposed naturalistic philosophy and is not a scientific hypothesis such that we can even imagine what could constitute falsification of it if it is false.

DAVID: Well I don't really mind whether Popper would classify it as a scientific hypothesis or not. It's a theory, if you like, whether scientific or philosophical. It's obvious to me that our mental life is totally dependent upon the operation of our physical brains. This is what most people in our society today believe.

JOHN: Our mental life may, as you say, be dependent on our having physical brains. But that's not the same as saying that mental life is *identical with* brain activity. That idea comes from the naturalistic assumption that I'm afraid you share with so many others. But when pressed to its logical conclusion it becomes untenable.

DAVID: Oh, how so?

JOHN: Well suppose, as physicalism claims, that every event in the world is part of the universal causal system of nature. There may be an element of indeterminacy at the quantum level, but at the macro level of the world of which we are aware, including our brains, everything happens of necessity. So if physicalism, or materialism, is true there can be no intellectual free-will, but only causally determined thoughts, emotions and volitions. The point I want to make goes back to Epicurus when he said, 'He who says that all things happen of necessity cannot criticize another who says that not all things happen of necessity. For he has to admit that the assertion also happens of necessity.'[8]

DAVID: That's if you're thinking in terms of what is called libertarian, or non-compatibilist, freedom. But I don't believe there is any such thing. The reality is a freedom that is compatible with our being totally determined. Everything that we do is causally determined, although it seems to us that we are free.

JOHN: Certainly it seems to us that we are free. But let us suppose that the physical world is in fact completely determined. It is then the case that some of us are causally determined to believe that complete determinism obtains while others are causally determined to believe the contrary. Can those who are right in believing that they are totally determined ever *know* or rationally believe this?

DAVID: What are you getting at?

JOHN: Well, imagine a non-determined mind observing our world from outer space. She can think freely, direct her attention at will, weigh up evidence and arguments, and form her own judgements. Let us suppose she observes that our world, including ourselves, is a completely determined system. But while she can see that we on earth are all completely determined, she knows it in a different sense of 'know' from that in which those of you who correctly believe this nevertheless know it. So if there are, or could be, non-determined intellectual volitions, a non-determined mind can rationally hold beliefs in a sense in which a totally determined mind/brain never can. In other words, if we are all causally determined to believe what we believe, there are no freely arrived at judgements – not even your own judgement about compatibilist freedom.

DAVID: I think the determinist might have a reply to this. He is saying in effect that our brains are biological computers, producing conclusions in a totally logical way, so that the determinist may nevertheless be determined in such a way that he arrives at a true conclusion.

JOHN: Yes, its true that we *may* be totally determined, and that we *may* happen to be determined to believe the truth. But if so, none of us can rationally believe this. Two people debating the question would be like two computers functioning in accordance with their different programmes, with only a non-determined outside observer being able to tell which of them is programmed to arrive at the truth.

DAVID: Okay. But there's another suggestion that I've heard. Perhaps the ultimate programmer is the world itself in which true beliefs aid survival, so that in the course of evolution wrongly programmed brains have been eliminated while correctly programmed ones survive. In that case the process whereby our brains have become efficient truth-seekers is a strictly natural phenomenon.

JOHN: Yes. But there is a problem here too. Why would a totally determined biological computer arrive at the species-wide delusion that it is not determined? The delusion would have to have survival value. How could it, if we are simply totally determined computers? We do what we are caused to do, and consciousness, whether deluded or not, adds nothing.

DAVID: Actually, I am inclined to agree with you so long as we are talking about libertarian, or non-compatibilist, freedom. But as I said before I reject that as unreal and affirm compatibilist freedom – a freedom that is compatible with our being totally determined. We are determined by a multitude of circumstances, and above all by our genes.

JOHN: No, we are not entirely determined by circumstances, or by our genes. As someone has said, 'Genes are like the keys of a piano: they determine what possibilities are available, but leave the pianist free to make his or her own music.' And the same is true of circumstances. But it looks as though we are going to have to agree to disagree about that.

9
More on Neuroscience

DAVID: Quite apart from that, I'm still not satisfied. There are so many ways in which physical causes can produce religious experiences. I mentioned earlier the Persinger helmet, which induces religious visions in some people. And the fact that epileptic seizures sometimes likewise involve religious visions and voices. You quoted earlier from William James's *Varieties of Religious Experience*. Do you remember the bit where he describes his own experience when experimenting with nitrous oxide. He said that it can

> stimulate the mystic consciousness to an extraordinary degree. Depth upon depth of truth seems revealed to the inhaler. This truth fades out, however, or escapes, at the moment of coming to; and if any words remain over in which it seemed to clothe itself, they prove to be the veriest nonsense.[1]

And coming closer to some of the kinds of religious experience that you cited earlier, Ray Jordan, experimenting with a low dosage of LSD, reported,

I have realized that quite literally everything is Self, everything in the whole field of experience – both what is usually known as self and all that is usually not self (people, objects, sky, earth, etc.). This Self, which is everything is not the same as the ego-self. It is not that I, Ray Jordan, am everything, but that there is a more fundamental self which is everything, including Ray Jordan.[2]

This sounds very like Hindu mystical experience. And doesn't it show that changes to the chemistry of the brain can induce what you call religious experience?

JOHN: No surely not, any more than the fact that, by using a telescope, we can induce the seeing of craters on the moon shows that there are no craters on the moon. What we're calling inducing an experience may produce an illusion or it may enable us to become aware of something that's already there. So if the transcendent reality of which the religions speak is there, there may be both spontaneous awareness of it and also awareness made possible by the effect on us of religious symbols, rituals, music, and also of some brain altering drugs.

DAVID: So obviously the churches should distribute cannabis at their communion services – like *soma* in the Solidarity Services in Aldous Huxley's *Brave New World*!

JOHN: Touché. Unfortunately there's also an important negative side to using drugs in this context. Religious experience induced by drugs is typically transient in its effects unless it occurs within the long-term transformation of the personality through a prolonged discipline of prayer or meditation within a whole life increasingly oriented to the Transcendent. It may constitute a glimpse which only momentarily affects one's life, as distinguished from a longer and deeper awareness that is integrated into a spiritually receptive mind and form of life. The great mystics of all traditions have always developed a holistic spirituality which involves their whole lives, not just temporary 'highs' provided by drugs or any other means.

DAVID: Okay. But now I want to bring in some interesting work that you referred to yourself earlier, done by Andrew Newberg when he reported the results of scans on eight meditators in the Tibetan Buddhist tradition who cooperated with him in his research. When after a certain period of time they signalled that they had achieved the inner state they were seeking, he injected into their blood stream a radioactive tracer that can be detected by the SPECT[3] machine, showing increased and decreased blood flow to different areas of the brain. He found in each case a sharply decreased blood flow to the mass of neurons called the posterior superior parietal lobe, the primary function of which is orientation in space, including the distinction between self and environment; and he concluded that the meditators' sense of unity with the universe reflected this[4] – in other words, that the decreased blood flow caused the mystical experience.

JOHN: Yes, but one could equally well conclude that it was the Tibetan monks' deliberate effort in meditation, achieved after many years of practice, that caused the decreased flow of blood to that particular area of the brain, where it was not now needed. And more generally, that it was the deliberate openness of religious meditators to the universal presence of the Transcendent that causes these various cerebral changes.

DAVID: Theoretically perhaps.

JOHN: There's further support for this in James Austin's massive book, *Zen and the Brain*. He found that the practice over a number of years of zazen, the distinctive Zen method of meditation, modifies brain structure and function and makes possible a new form of consciousness and indeed of self. He says that the experience of *satori* or *kensho*, that is, profound far-reaching enlightenment, is already there as a potentiality in the structure of the brain, as 'innate, existing brain functions, [which can be] rearranged into new configurations'.[5] There is a resulting sense of unity with the totality of reality, a complete absence of any kind of anxiety, worry or fear, a focused 'mindfulness' and a serenity and kindliness in relation to others. Austin distinguishes between the pragmatic ego, which is 'each person's capacity to deal confidently with life in a mature, realistic, matter-of-fact way',[6] which is not lessened but on the contrary strengthened by zazen, and the negative ego, the selfish self which he says, 'Zen trainees first need to define, identify, and then work through. Not in ways that crush or deny their essential natural selves, but in ways that will simultaneously encourage the flow of their basic ethical, compassionate impulses.'[7] They are recovering what Buddhism calls the true or original self, which is our ultimate Buddha nature, now overlaid by the pervasive influences of our ego-deluded human society.

DAVID: Yes, Zen masters, and people like the Dalai Lama, are impressive, I admit. But that doesn't *prove* anything. But, incidentally, have you ever met any of them?

JOHN: Actually, yes. I have met and had long conversations with three roshis, or Zen masters, two of whom were heads of large monasteries in Kyoto, and one who taught in Tokyo. And it is true that while, on the one hand, they had transcended to a considerable extent their natural self-centredness, on the other, their 'pragmatic ego' was extremely powerful.

But to come back to the basic issue: does neurophysiology describe the neural *correlates* of mental states, leaving open the question of which is causing which at particular moments, or does it by describing these neural correlates give a naturalistic explanation of all mental activity?

DAVID: I believe the latter. We have to be concerned with reality, and for me that means the physical universe. Science just doesn't leave any space for the non-physical, the suprasensory or supranatural.

JOHN: But surely consciousness itself is non-physical? And if the inner life of consciousness is non-physical, doesn't this at least open up the possibility that it connects with a larger nonsensory reality?

DAVID: No doubt it would. But that possibility doesn't arise, because consciousness simply is neural activity. It consists without remainder in the electro-chemical functioning of the brain.

JOHN: And I've already explained why I think this is not the case. Let me put it once more in some words of John Oman, writing about the 'emergence' of mind from matter, 'This is as much as to say that a signpost turns into a policeman when the traffic becomes complex enough to need him.'[8] But once again it seems that we can only agree to disagree.

DAVID: Indeed. But nevertheless I'm curious about something else. Although you have been defending religion I'm pretty sure that your ideas must be anathema to the churches. What do your ideas imply for Christianity?

10
Implications for Christianity

DAVID: Although I want to hear about the implications of your position for Christianity, since I'm not a Christian I've asked my friend Grace, who describes herself as an ordinary churchgoing Christian, to join us. I've told her about your suggestion that the different religions are different human responses, in different human terms, to the same ultimate transcendent reality, and I think she wonders if this is compatible with Christianity.

JOHN: Good. Hello, Grace. Good to meet you. I gather you're worried about what my philosophy means for my Christianity.

GRACE: Yes, John. You were, after all, an ordained minister of the United Reformed Church until you became a Quaker, and so still a Christian. In fact I believe you started your Christian life with a powerful evangelical conversion?

JOHN: Yes I did.

GRACE: Tell me a bit more about it.

JOHN: It was when I was a young Law student, intending to follow in the family tradition by becoming a solicitor and carrying on the small provincial firm begun by my grandfather and by then led by my father. I think I was always religiously, or spiritually, inclined in a vague sort of way, although totally bored by the church services that I had to go to as a child. But now for several days, under the impact of the New Testament figure of Jesus, I was in a state of intense mental and emotional turmoil. I was increasingly aware of what seemed to be a higher truth and greater reality pressing in on me and claiming my recognition and response. At first this was highly unwelcome, a disturbing and challenging demand for nothing less than a revolution in my personal identity. But then the disturbing claim became a liberating invitation. The reality that was pressing upon me was not only awesomely demanding but also irresistibly attractive, and I entered with great joy and excitement into the world of Christian faith.

GRACE: And did this bring with it the ordinary Christian beliefs?

JOHN: More than ordinary – ordinary with knobs on! The fellow students I was among, who had led me to reread the Gospels, were members of the evangelical student movement, the Inter-Varsity Fellowship, and throwing in my lot with them I took over the whole fundamentalist theological package – the verbal inspiration of the scriptures, seven day creation and the fall of Adam and Eve, Jesus as God incarnate, his virgin birth, miracles, redemption only by his death on the cross, his bodily resurrection and ascension into heaven – the whole lot. I must have been a terrible bore to most of my friends and family. But it now seemed natural to switch from the Law to prepare for the Christian ministry, in my case in the Presbyterian Church of England because that was the church to which my friends belonged – this later united with the majority of the Congregationalists to form the United Reformed Church.

GRACE: And you were, I believe, in due course ordained and served as minister of a church in Northumberland. But what was it that made you later doubt your evangelical beliefs?

JOHN: These were the days of the so-called 'learned ministry' and as the first part of my theological training I had to take a university degree, which I did in Edinburgh in philosophy. Philosophy, of course, teaches you to ask questions. I was a member of the Evangelical Union at Edinburgh, but when I began to ask such obvious and simple questions as What should we make of the story that the sun stood still for about twenty-four hours to give the Israelites more time to slay the Amorites, as described in the Old Testament?[1] this was treated as 'backsliding'. However, while gradually ceasing to be a full-blooded fundamentalist I did remain basically conservative, theologically, for a number of years. It took a long time to detach myself from it.

GRACE: And how far have you now moved? Do you accept the central Christian belief in Jesus as Son of God, second person of the Trinity?

JOHN: No.

GRACE: But why not?

JOHN: I don't think that Jesus himself, the historical figure, taught it or believed it. I see it as something which the Church gradually developed after his death.

GRACE: But didn't Jesus say, 'I and my father are one'[2] and 'He who has seen me has seen the Father'[3] and 'I am the way, and the truth, and the life',[4] and 'Before Abraham was, I am'[5]?

JOHN: No, almost certainly not. These sayings all come from St John's Gospel, which the great majority of New Testament scholars believe was the last to be written, sometime in the 90s up to the end of the first century, some seventy years after Jesus' time and expressing the still developing beliefs of the writer's part of the Church at that time. They cannot be attributed to the historical Jesus himself.

GRACE: You say, his part of the Church. But surely the Church was all one.

JOHN: Well no, in those early days after Christianity had spread out beyond Judaism there was no central organization or authority. Different churches used different books, and some of the earliest manuscripts include books which are not in the present version of the New Testament. Probably the beginning was a collection of Paul's letters, which came before the Gospels, and then later the Gospels and the other documents were added. Actually the process of fixing the official contents of the New Testament took several centuries. The earliest known list of the contents as we have them now comes from bishop Athanasius of Alexandria in 367.

GRACE: But going back to those sayings of Jesus, why should the fact that they are in John's Gospel make any difference?

JOHN: It's because of the difference between John and the other three Gospels, Matthew, Mark and Luke. Mark is believed to have been written in about 70, forty years after the death of Jesus, Matthew and Luke in the 80s, and John, as I said, in the 90s. The first three are called the Synoptic Gospels because they share quite a lot of material, Matthew and Luke being in effect enlarged editions of Mark, but using further material of their own, and also possibly a lost document called Q – short for the German *Quelle*, source – though this last is disputed by a number of scholars. In the Synoptics Jesus often teaches in short pithy sayings and in his marvellous parables of the love of God. And he makes no claim to be divine. Indeed he is reported in Mark as saying on one occasion, 'Why do you call me good? No one is good but God alone.'[6] In John's Gospel, in contrast, he teaches in long theological discourses, quite different in both style and content from his teaching in the Synoptics, only once using a parable,[7] if indeed it is a parable, and he does make explicit claims to be divine. This is why most scholars believe that the Synoptics are closer to the Jesus of history as distinguished from the later Christ of faith. But it is the Christ of faith, superseding the historical Jesus, whom the Church has inherited in its developed belief-system.

GRACE: But what about Jesus' virgin birth? Doesn't that make him divine?

JOHN: By Jesus' virgin birth we mean, strictly speaking, his virginal conception, and this is told by both Matthew and Luke in the 80s. It doesn't seem to have been known to the earlier Christian writers, Paul – who wrote in the 50s – or Mark, nor is it referred to by any other New Testament writers, John, Peter, James, Jude or the author of Revelation. So the story first appears in writing eighty or more years after the supposed event, and in very different forms in Matthew and Luke. I am inclined, as are many others, to see it as a legend of the kind that developed around a number of figures in the ancient world. In fact stories of miraculous conceptions occur very widely – in the cultures of the ancient Egyptians, Greeks, Persians and Indians. As a major example, there was a legend of this kind attached to the birth of the Buddha.

GRACE: Really? I didn't know that.

JOHN: Yes, really. So it's not surprising that Christianity also produced its virgin birth story, although, as in Buddhism, in the modern world it has come to be widely seen, at least in the scholarly world, as legend rather than history.

GRACE: Nevertheless, it's in the creed we recite at church and I shall go on believing in Jesus, 'born of the virgin Mary'. But apart from that, surely Jesus' resurrection shows very clearly his divine nature?

JOHN: This is a big and enormously contentious subject. Most people, when they hear passages from the Gospels read in church, see them as all part of a single narrative. But in fact there are two different narratives, one telling of a bodily resurrection and the other of visions of Jesus after his death. Let's start with the first Gospel, Mark. The earliest manuscripts end half way through the last chapter, at verse 8, with the women finding the empty tomb and a young man there telling them that Jesus will appear to the disciples in Galilee; and the Gospel ends, 'And they went out and fled from the tomb; for trembling and astonishment had come upon them; and they said nothing to anyone, for they were afraid'. All the rest of the chapter, from verse 9 onwards, was added a few decades later by someone else, presumably because the original ending was so unsatisfactory – unsatisfactory, that is, from the point of view of the later Gospel writers.

GRACE: But what about Matthew and Luke?

JOHN: They both follow Mark as far as the empty tomb but then tell quite different and incompatible stories. According to Luke two disciples meet Jesus on the nearby Emmaeus road, although they only recognize him as being Jesus at the last moment, over a meal, at which point he disappears. These two disciples then go back and tell the others and Jesus suddenly appears to them all in a room where they were all keeping safely out of sight. He shows his wounds to prove that this was his bodily presence, and then leads them outside to Bethany where he is taken up into heaven. All this happens in Jerusalem and its environs the same day. And in Acts – also written by Luke – everything happens in Jerusalem and ends with Jesus' bodily ascension into heaven. In this Jerusalem tradition there are the curious features that the disciples on the Emmaus road do not recognize the man they are talking to as Jesus, and also that Jesus is able suddenly to disappear and later to appear in a closed room. But there are no appearances in Galilee, as promised in Mark.

Another curious point is that if, according to Luke, Jesus was able to pass through walls, and to appear and disappear at will, why should the stone have had to be rolled away from the door of the tomb, as Mark and Matthew say? Would it not have been much stronger evidence of the resurrection if the tomb had remained sealed and guarded by soldiers and then officially opened and found to be empty? Anyway, that's Luke.

Matthew, in contrast, has no appearances in Jerusalem but instead has Jesus appearing to the disciples in Galilee, but again with the curious addition that 'some doubted'[8] or, as another possible translation, some wondered. And there is no ascension. But there is something else very curious in Matthew. He says that at the time of Jesus' resurrection many dead bodies came out of their tombs and entered Jerusalem and were seen by many.[9] This reminds us of two things. One is that in the Judaism of that time resurrection, meaning a future resurrection of faithful Jews, naturally meant bodily resurrection, so that if there had been stories of visions of Jesus these could very easily almost two generations later have become the story that he had been bodily resurrected.

And the other point is that it shows us what Matthew's readers could be expected to believe without question. In the ancient world, unlike today, miracle stories were common and relatively easily believed. People usually didn't ask for the evidence. If someone told them of a miracle they usually had no difficulty in believing it.

Sorry to have gone on so long, but there is a lot to say about this.

GRACE: That's all right. I must admit that I hadn't noticed all that. It is troubling, but I'm sure there must be scholars who defend the physical resurrection.

JOHN: Yes, there are. One of their main arguments is that something very remarkable must have happened to the first disciples to change a group of sad and frightened men into the confident apostles who launched a movement which has grown to include more than a third of the world's population.

GRACE: And could anything less than Jesus being among them again after his crucifixion and burial have been enough to do that?

JOHN: I certainly agree that something very remarkable must have happened. The question is, what was it that happened? At this point let's bring in St Paul. He was writing his letters in the 50s, much earlier than the Gospels. After listing Jesus' appearances to the first disciples Paul says, 'Last of all, as to someone untimely born, he appeared also to me.'[10] It was this that made him an apostle, equally with the others. In his letters he does not describe Jesus' appearing to him, but in the Acts of the Apostles there are two accounts. In one Paul is speaking to a Jewish audience about his dramatic conversion from a persecutor of Christians:

> While I was on my way and approaching Damascus, about noon a great light from heaven suddenly shone about me. I fell to the ground and heard a voice saying to me, 'Saul, Saul, why are you persecuting me?' I answered, 'Who are you, Lord?' Then he said to me, 'I am Jesus of Nazareth whom you are persecuting.' Now those who were with me saw the light but did not hear the voice of the one who was speaking to me.[11]

Later, speaking to king Agrippa, Paul describes his experience again, with his companions again not hearing the voice. So it was evidently an inner voice, heard only by Paul. But in neither account is there the bodily presence of Jesus – if there had been, his companions would also have seen it. So, since Paul says elsewhere that Jesus had appeared to him, this appearing must have consisted in a vision of Jesus – but an inner vision, because no one else saw it. This is the earliest account we have of the experience that came to be called seeing the risen Jesus. And so my own conclusion is that very probably the original resurrection experiences of the disciples were of the same kind: they saw visions of Jesus after his death.

GRACE: Well, you could be right, though I hope not. And surely I remember reading in Acts that after his conversion and his visit to Damascus Paul went to Jerusalem to meet the apostles who told him their message, which was that Christ died for our sins, was buried, then appeared to Peter and then to the rest of the twelve. And then – this is in Paul's first letter to the Corinthians – 'he appeared to more than five hundred brothers and sisters at one time, most of whom are still alive, though some have died'.[12] Now surely an appearance to five hundred people at once can't be a vision. It must have been bodily.

JOHN: Yes indeed. But if such a startling thing really happened why is it not mentioned in any of the Gospels? But the first question is whether this report of the five hundred is part of what Paul received from the apostles. His visit to Jerusalem will have been two or three years after his conversion, which would have been another two or three years after Jesus' death in 30, for the growing Jesus movement quickly came to be seen as a dangerous heresy by orthodox Judaism, and one which Paul, then Saul, felt called to combat. Now after five or six years most of any five hundred people would still be alive. It therefore seems unlikely that the reference to the five hundred was part of the apostles' original message to Paul, and much more likely that it was a development of the story that had come about by the time Paul was writing, some twenty years later, in the 50s, and which he added in at this point.

GRACE: All that strikes me as speculation rather than certainty.

JOHN: Yes, I'm afraid almost everything anyone says about events nearly two thousand years ago has to fall short of certainty. All that we can really say is that some reconstructions seem more probable than others. But there is another reason for doubting whether Paul, when he spoke of the risen lord appearing to him, meant a physical resurrection. For in one of his letters he says, 'It is sown a physical body, it is raised a spiritual body. If there is a physical body, there is also a spiritual body', and 'flesh and blood cannot inherit the kingdom'.[13] So I still think that it is most likely that both Paul and some of the original apostles had visions of Jesus after his death. After all, visions of people who have died are not all that uncommon.

GRACE: Really? Do you know of any?

JOHN: Yes. I once had such a vision myself. My youngest son, when he was only 24, died in a mountain accident in the Alps. A few weeks later I had a sudden brief vision of him standing beside me and then going away through some kind of door, with the feeling that this was alright. And I've heard of several other people who have had visions of their loved ones who had died.

GRACE: I'm truly sorry to hear of the tragedy of your son's death. So there can be such visions; but of course it doesn't follow that the resurrection appearances were like that. As you put it, it's all a matter of 'probably' and 'most likely', and that's not enough to shake my faith in the story as we believe it in church.

JOHN: Nor do I want to shake your faith, but only to raise questions to think about. And so I add one last question, Do you want to base your belief on the shifting sands of the sort of considerations I've been describing, reducing it to a probability judgement, or would you rather decide to ignore all the problems we've been discussing? And can you really live with that, suppressing the problems?

GRACE: The situation is really more complex than that, John. When I go to church we say the creed, but I don't think most of us really bother much about what it means. They're more a declaration of belonging to a two-thousand-year-old tradition. And we sing the hymns, which between them probably have quite a lot of verses that you would object to, but again we don't really think very much about that. And when the lessons are read from the Old and New Testaments we don't, as you said, compare one Gospel with another. We don't get into what they call biblical criticism. Again, the sermons are usually about more immediate matters, about the world around us and about how to live. So in practice the problems you've been pointing to don't usually bother us. I go to church because I get some real uplift from the atmosphere, the music, the words, and I meet my friends, I'm part of a community, and I don't think most of us bother too much about theology. No doubt the priest does. But that's his business.

JOHN: Yes, I can understand that and I can respect it. And of course I know that many churches do a great deal of good in their neighbourhood and in supporting charities. Although I criticize the churches' official beliefs, and want these to change fairly radically, I have no quarrel with my many friends who are churchgoers. And many thanks for joining us today.

DAVID: Yes, thanks from me too, Grace. So, John, the implications of your philosophy for Christianity are that its belief system should be pretty radically changed, particularly in abandoning its central belief in Jesus as God incarnate. Correct?

JOHN: Yes, what in my view has gradually to be winnowed out is the implied claim to unique superiority over all other religions. You see, if Jesus was God incarnate – or God the Son, second person of a divine Trinity – this means that Christianity alone among the religions of the world was founded by God in person. God came down from heaven to earth in the person of Jesus to found a new religion – Christianity. But that is not possible if the global interpretation of religion I was outlining, or anything like it, is correct.

DAVID: So presumably the same general principle – no unique superiority – applies to all the other religions as well?

JOHN: Correct.

DAVID: I'd like to hear a little more about how that plays out, particularly in the case of Islam.

11
Implications for Islam

DAVID: As I said, the other religion that I'd particularly like us to look at is Islam, which is so much in the news today – suicide bombers, oppressive shariah laws and so on. You say that your philosophy of global religion has implications for this too?

JOHN: Yes, its implications are very much in tune with what today's reformers within Islam are proposing.

DAVID: So there are reformers within Islam. But it is generally held that Islam worldwide is today in a low state.

JOHN: Yes, and I think that's right, even though numerically the religion is growing. But I'm sure that an Islamic renaissance is on it's way, because there are already early renaissance figures like the early renaissance thinkers in the West many centuries ago.

DAVID: And who are today's early renaissance figures in the Islamic world?

JOHN: Two of the earliest were Sir Muhammad Iqbal in what is now Pakistan and Mohamed Taha early in the twentieth century in the Sudan. But today enlightened thinking crops up all over the Muslim world: the other day the Grand Mufti of Lebanon said very sensibly that just as Jesus was neither a Catholic nor a Protestant, so also Muhammad was neither a Sunni nor a Shia. Among the academics there are Mohamed Arkoun in France, Ali Ashgar Engineer in India, Mohamed Talbi in Tunisia, Mahmut Aydin in Turkey, Fuzlur Rahman in the United States, Farid Esack in South Africa, Tariq Ramadan in Britain, and Muslim feminists such as Amina Wadud, and Fatima Mermissa in Morocco, Mahmoud Ayoub in the United States, and perhaps most importantly Abdolkarim Soroush of Iran but now teaching in the United States.

DAVID: And why is he the most important?

JOHN: He's possibly the most radical, the one who has come to grips most directly with the central problems. In the early days of the Iranian revolution, when the Shah was overthrown, he supported Ayatollah Khomeini and acted as an advisor on cultural and educational reform. But later he became disappointed with the idea of an Islamic theocracy and began to advocate democracy in Iran. He was listed in 2005 by *Time* magazine as one of the hundred most influential people in the world. He is a practising Muslim, with both a scientific and a theological training. He has written extensively in Persian – or Farsi – although only two volumes of his writings have so far been translated into English.

DAVID: So let's take him as our window into what you say is a budding Islamic renaissance.

JOHN: Or better, an advocate of reform leading hopefully towards a future renaissance. Well, one of the things that Soroush says is that the prophet Muhammad's experience of revelation was not unique in nature, but was the 'paradigm case' (4)[1] of religious experience. I would not myself say that it was *the* but rather *a* paradigm case, others being the experiences of Jesus and of Gautama the Buddha. But the important thing that this leads to, according to Soroush, is that the revelations that became the Qur'an were of necessity mediated through a human mind formed within a particular human culture at a particular point in history, and expressed in a particular human language embodying its own conceptual structure. Further,

> The message of the revelation also changed depending on the context. In Mecca, the Prophet's task was to shake people up, to alarm and awaken them. It was his business to smash the old dogmas. He therefore needed piercing and penetrating sermons and decisive ideological stances. But in Medina, it was time for construction, for following through the mission, for consolidating the teaching. Here what was needed was legislation and lengthy, all-encompassing explanations and dialogue with the people. Of course, the Prophet's endurance for religious and prophetic experience had also grown. Hence, the form and content of the message also changed. This is the norm with any experience, that it should grow and mature. (11)

DAVID: There's quite a lot here that you will have to explain, because it presupposes a knowledge of history that I don't have. What was all that about Mecca and Medina, and why did people in Mecca need to be shaken up?

JOHN: To start at the beginning, Muhammad was born about 570 CE in Mecca in Arabia – now Saudi

Arabia – and made his living as a merchant and formerly a shepherd. He married at the age of 25. Arabia was a place of tribes, often at war with one another, and the people were polytheists, worshipping a number of gods. Because of its huge shrine, the Kaaba, Mecca was a place of pilgrimage, bringing a good deal of wealth to the place. But when he was 40 Muhammad, feeling that something was profoundly wrong with the culture, retreated to a cave outside Mecca to meditate, and it was then that he received his first revelatory experience. This was essentially that God is one. There are no gods, only God, the Arabic 'Allah' meaning 'the God' – hence the Muslim profession of faith, 'There is no god but God.' And true worship is islam with a small i, which means submission – to God.

DAVID: This was new?

JOHN: Yes, and it was a dangerous message in Mecca at that time. It meant that the many gods had to be denied, and the shrine on which a good deal of the economy depended cleansed. The pilgrimages would end and the city suffer. The Meccan establishment reacted so strongly against this that Muhammad and his group of followers had to leave Mecca, in peril for their lives, and go to Medina. This move is called the Hijra and Islamic history is dated from then. And in Medina Muhammad set up a Muslim community to, in the words of the Qur'an, 'establish prayers and welfare of the poor and shall command good and forbid evil' (22:40). This new community had its own laws.

DAVID: And what about these laws? I believe they're called the shariah and they include cutting off a thief's hand, stoning an adulterer – man or woman – to death, and polygamy. And a woman's evidence in court counts for only half a man's; and a husband can divorce his wife merely by saying so, but not vice versa.

JOHN: Yes, that's right. Though we need to be aware of the nuances: for example, in order to establish adultery there have to be four witnesses – which, obviously, there hardly ever are. And today very few Muslim countries practise these punishments and discriminations – in fact, only Saudi Arabia, which is dominated by a particular school of Muslim thought, the Deobandis. In Pakistan, the situation varies. There have been attempts to practise the full rigour of the punishments, though at the same time, in a 1961 law, polygamy and male-pronounced divorce were made difficult, though not illegal. All this is in contrast to Bangladesh, the other Muslim country on the Indian sub-continent, where none of this is practised. Likewise in Indonesia, which has the largest Muslim population in the world, a gentler form of Islam is practised, influenced by the Sufi missionaries who first brought the faith there.

DAVID: Sufis. Who are they?

JOHN: The Sufis are the mystics within Islam. They believe that it is possible, by purifying the self of egoism, to experience the presence of God – like the mystics of other religions. One of the most famous was Rumi, who lived in the thirteenth century CE, on whom Dr Soroush is an authority. It was Rumi who spoke about the religions of the world, saying, 'The lamps are different but the Light is the same; it comes from Beyond.'[2] It is this spirit of toleration and acceptance of difference that today pervades Muslim societies influenced by Sufism.

DAVID: Okay. So, going back to Soroush, has he been influenced by Sufism?

JOHN: Yes, clearly so. But he believes that Muhammad himself was not a mystic but a prophet, a prophet being one who not only experiences the divine presence but also is convinced that he is commanded by God to proclaim a message and to change the world. He emphasizes that Muhammad was a very human vehicle of revelation, growing in his capacity to understand God's will. Soroush paraphrases a verse in the Qur'an (25:32) as saying,

> We shall reveal the Qur'an to you gradually so that you may gain in confidence, so that you may become sturdier and more resolute, so that you may not be overawed and troubled by doubts, so that the opposition and enmity that you face does not undermine your resolve, so that you may know that you are Prophet. (9)

Soroush summarizes what he has to say about the human reception of revelation through Muhammad by saying that it came in

> a particular language, particular concepts and particular methods (*fiqh*[3] and ethics). All this occurs in a particular time and place (geographical and cultural) and for a particular people with particular physical and mental capacities. [The Prophet] is faced with specific reactions and questions and, in response to them gives specific answers. The flow of religion over the course of time in turn gives rise to events, moving some people to acquiesce and

others to repudiate. Believers and unbelievers fall into particular relationships with each other and religion; they fight battles or create civilisations, engage in comprehending and expanding religious ideas and experiences or wrecking and undermining them. (90–1).

And all this has important practical implications for Muslims today.

DAVID: Such as?

JOHN: Soroush distinguishes between essentials and accidentals in religion, and identifies the accidentals in the case of Islam. One is the Arabic language. He points out that 'It would have been enough for the Prophet of Islam to have been born an Iranian, an Indian or a Roman for his language to become Persian, Sanskrit or Latin' (70). He likens a language to a flute – the flute player can play whatever tune he likes on the flute, but only within the limits imposed by the nature of the flute. So the Arabic language has its own unique character and rhythm and metaphors.

And then a second accidental is the Arab culture of Muhammad's time – its desert provenance, its customs, world-view and traditions. As he says,

> The fact that the Qur'an speaks of the presence in heaven of dark-eyed *houris* (not blue-eyed women) and portrayed them as sheltered in their tents (55:72); that it calls on people to consider how the camel was created (88:17); that it refers to warm-weather fruits with which the Arabs were acquainted ... that it uses the lunar calendar ... that it describes the presence in heaven of 'uplifted couches and goblets set forth and cushions arrayed and carpets outspread' (88:14–16) ... all reveal how the hue

and scent of Arabs' interests, sensibilities, tribal life, violence, hospitality, customs, habits, surroundings and
livelihoods have enveloped the central kernel of Islamic
thought like a hefty shell. (701)

Again, the key words of the Qur'an, not only 'Allah'
but many more,

belonged to the Arabs and were products of their culture and world-view. Nonetheless, within Islam and with
reference to the new source of authority, they took on a
new spirit and hue. In other words, the Prophet of Islam
used the bricks at his disposal within Arab culture to
construct a new structure, which is related to that culture
but also surpasses it. (73)

And Soroush gives a number of other examples of
the way in which the Qur'an is rooted in an Arab
culture whose people were people of commerce and
of the desert.

DAVID: Yes, all that certainly makes sense. So it seems
that he relativizes Islam?

JOHN: No, it would be misleading to say that. He relativizes the accidentals of Islam – and indeed of every
religion – but thereby reveals its essential core, which
is the oneness of God and *islam,* obedience to God.
Soroush says:

There can be no doubt that, had Islam come into existence in Greece or India, instead of in Hijaz, the accidentals of Greek or Indian Islam – accidentals which penetrate
so deep as to touch the kernel – would have been very
different from those of an Arab Islam. The powerful

ideas of Greek philosophy, for example, would have provided the Prophet of Islam with different linguistic tools
and a different word system that would have altered his
discourse; in much the same way as we can see that,
today, after centuries of travels and travails, Iranian,
Indian, Arab and Indonesian Islam are very different in
the testimony of their religious literature (as well as having many similarities), and not just in appearance but
to the very depth of their religious understanding and
culture. (77)

Another respect in which the Qur'anic revelation
was affected by the culture of the time is the scientific
knowledge that it presupposes. Yet again, 'the Qur'an
could have been shorter or longer than it is and
still have been the Qur'an, because it is the Qur'an
by virtue of its essentials, not its accidentals' (81).
As Soroush says, 'The entry of these accidentals into
religion reveal its dynamic interlocutory nature. They
demonstrate the way in which this religion moved in
step with events of the time and the Prophet's actual
experiences ... '(81).

DAVID: Very sensible. But what about the shariah laws –
the floggings, hand chopping and all that sort of
thing. Is this, according to Soroush, essential or accidental? Does it belong to the core of Islam, or can it
be abandoned?

JOHN: According to Soroush it is an accidental,
derived from the culture and needs of the time, not
part of the core of Islam. He refers to the cutting of
a thief's hand as an example of the mistaken 'maxi-
malist' view that traditional religion is perfect and
contains everything necessary for a happy afterlife.

In contrast to this he advocates a 'minimalist' view according to which:

> We must, instead, concentrate entirely on their this-worldly success in resolving problems and, wherever the precepts of *fiqh* [shariah] do not yield the desired results in today's complex, industrial societies (on issues such as commerce, matrimony, banking, rent, theft, talion [legal retaliation], governance, politics and so on), we must change them. In other words, *fiqh* will become an earthly and pragmatic legal science, which is constantly added to or subtracted from in the light of pragmatic considerations. (98–9)

Incidentally, Soroush has developed some of this further in the other book of his that is available in English, *Reason, Freedom, and Democracy in Islam*.[4] But going back to hand chopping, in an interview included in his book he says quite explicitly that

> Some parts of religion are historically and culturally determined and no longer relevant today. That is the case, for instance, with the corporal punishments prescribed in the Koran. If the prophet had lived in another cultural environment, those punishments would probably not have been part of his message. (275)

DAVID: I like all that. But what do other Muslims think about this? Are his reforming proposals acceptable more widely?

JOHN: Unfortunately not. Soroush's book includes in an appendix an exchange of letters with the Iranian Ayatollah Sobhani. Some of Sobhani's words are quite harsh. For example,

Dr Soroush in his previous discussion (on the subject of the Imamate and the caliphate) was unkind to the Sh'i Imams, but, here, he has gone a step further and been unkind to the realm of revelation and the Qur'an. I ask God to stop him here and not allow him to take another step, lest his felicity in the next world (which I am sure he seriously wants) is further endangered. (278)

He also speaks of Soroush's 'wild and unseemly remarks' (283), and says that 'By presenting the Qur'an as a fallible human book, you have distanced yourself from the Islamic community' (286). All this reminds me of the kind of language used by Christian fundamentalists to people like myself!

But it is true that Soroush's position is highly controversial and rejected by many, in fact most Muslims. The Whahabis in Saudi Arabia would probably regard it as blasphemy. But the majority of Muslims around the world are poor, ill-educated, many of them refugees struggling to survive – the per capita income of the Islamic world is only 10 per cent that of the West – and they have no time or inclination for philosophical discussion, and simply follow what their imams or mullahs tell them.

DAVID: He does indeed sound controversial. What would you say is his most controversial idea?

JOHN: I suppose it would be his idea, to which Ayatollah Sobhani refers, that Muhammad was the author of the Qur'an. He explains what he means by saying that revelation is inspiration.

It is the same experience as that of poets and mystics, although prophets are on a higher level. In our modern age we can understand revelation by using the metaphor of poetry ... The poet feels that he is informed by a source external to him; that he receives something. And poetry, just like revelation, is a talent ... What he [Muhammad] receives from God is the content of the revelation. This content, however, cannot be offered to the people as such, because it is beyond their understanding and even beyond words. It is formless and the activity of the person of the Prophet is to form the formless so as to make it accessible. Like a poet again, the Prophet transmits the inspiration in the language he knows, the styles he masters and the images and knowledge he possesses. (272–3)

DAVID: From which it seems to follow that the Qur'an is fallible.

JOHN: Soroush says in the same interview that

In the traditional view the revelation is infallible. But nowadays there are more and more interpreters who think that the revelation is infallible only in purely religious matters such as the attributes of God, life after death and the rules of worship ... What the Koran says about historical matters, other religious traditions and all kinds of practical earthly matters does not necessarily have to be true. (273)

Soroush believes that

It was his [Muhammad's] own language and his own knowledge and I don't think that he knew more than the people around him about the earth, the universe and the genetics of human beings. He did not possess the knowledge we have today. But that does not harm his prophethood because he was a prophet and not a scientist or a historian. (273–4)

DAVID: Certainly Soroush seems to be a very sensible and clear-thinking person, and I wish him well in his attempts to reform Islamic thought. But what about Islam on the ground today? What about the violence of the Taliban and al-Qaeda, the suicide bombers, the suppression of women and so on?

JOHN: Yes, this brings us to the wider question of the good and the harm done by religion, including of course Islam. Let's move on to that next.

12
The Religions: Good or Bad?

DAVID: Yes, I want now to look at religion on the ground, as it actually affects ordinary human life. I remember a BBC survey a few years ago, in which people were asked if they think that religion has done more harm than good; and 76 per cent said Yes, and 24 per cent No. And I'm inclined to join the 76 per cent. You remember what Grace was saying. But it's all very well for her to tell us, as she did, about the benefit she gets from going to church. I don't doubt that at all. But the kind of church she goes to is a pretty feeble example of the power that religion has had over the centuries, and still has in many parts of the world today. I want now to look at the bigger picture.

JOHN: Yes, I agree. But first of all, we have to distinguish between religion and the religions. Here I'm following Wilfred Cantwell Smith.

DAVID: Who is?

JOHN: Was – he died at a ripe old age in 2000. He was a Canadian scholar who founded and directed the Center for the Study of World Religions at Harvard.

He was enormously learned, using Sanscrit as well as Hebrew and Greek and several European languages. He had worked at one time in what is now Pakistan and was an authority on Islam as well as on the comparative study of religion globally. He was also the first major Western thinker to develop religious pluralism, the view that there is not just one but many true religions. In his classic book *The Meaning and End of Religion*[1] he distinguished between, on the one hand, the cumulative traditions, which include the religious organizations and their creeds, theologies and liturgies and, on the other hand, what he called faith – though I don't think that is the best word for it – by which he meant the individual response to the Transcendent. This is the inner experiential aspect of religion. The distinction is very important, because religious organizations by themselves have such a chequered history. In fact I would say that over the centuries they have done about equal amounts of good and bad in the world.

DAVID: What good of any real significance have the religions ever done?

JOHN: A lot. They've provided a framework of meaning, a grand narrative or overarching myth, for hundreds of millions of people; and they have been responsible for founding hospitals, schools, universities and so on; and they also meet our need for community, providing opportunities for people to come together and to collaborate in all sorts of ways that have benefited their societies.

DAVID: But surely, as you've admitted, they're also responsible for an enormous amount of evil. They have often been instruments of oppression, part of the power structure of nations, supporting crusades, being on both sides of every war, justifying slavery, the male oppression of women, the exploitation of the poor. And the more powerful they have been the more intolerant and brutal they have been, burning as heretics many who questioned the official dogmas, and burning thousands of women as witches, and generally suppressing freedom of thought and expression. As Pascal said, 'Men never do evil so completely and cheerfully as when they do it from religious conviction.'[2]

JOHN: Yes, all of that, and more. So the historical religious institutions cannot be described as direct responses to the Transcendent. They have originally come about through immensely influential individuals and then developed into communal responses to the Transcendent, but it's true that as they have developed they have increasingly become human, all-too-human. They are, if you like, a necessary evil – permanently necessary because we are communal beings. In secularized Europe today the churches are relatively harmless because they are relatively powerless. Indeed here their influence, though very limited, is almost wholly good. There is the beauty and deep appeal to some of liturgical worship, and the value of pastoral care for individuals in need, and public activities with their ripple effects in society.

DAVID: Yes, but where the churches are more powerful, in parts of the United States and in parts of Africa and South America, they do more harm. As you know, in the USA there is a strong correlation between right-wing religion and right-wing politics.

JOHN: Oh I don't dispute that at all.

DAVID: As something of a heretic yourself, as it seems, has this affected you?

JOHN: As a matter of fact, yes, though only compara-tively slightly. When I was in the United States, I taught at one time at Princeton Theological Seminary, which is Presbyterian. At that time I was a minister of the Presbyterian Church of England, which had not then become part of the United Reformed Church. When a Presbyterian – or URC – minister moves to a new place he automatically applies to join the local Presbytery, in this case the Presbytery of New Brunswick. It hap-pened that the chairman of the committee which received these applications was a deep-dyed funda-mentalist. He asked me when I met with the relevant committee if there was anything in the Westminster Confession of 1647, which was the church's official statement of belief, about which I had doubts. I began with the six days creation of the world; Adam and Eve and the Garden and Eden; the snake and the forbidden fruit; went on to the doctrine that God has preordained many to eternal torment in hell; and eventually got to the virgin birth – or rather virginal conception – of Jesus. This was something that I neither affirmed nor denied but did not identify with the central doctrine of the divinity of Christ, which at that time I still fully accepted. It was the virgin birth that ignited the chair-man's wrath. He was a disciple of J. Gresham Machen, author of *The Virgin Birth of Christ*, who in 1929 had founded his own super-conservative Westminster sem-inary. However, the Presbytery as a whole was satisfied that I should be accepted, which I duly was. But the chairman – Clyde Henry – and others then launched a Complaint to the next higher body, the Synod of New Jersey, which to our surprise and consternation upheld it. If this was allowed to stand I would lose my job, because professors at the Seminary had to be ministers of the United Presbyterian Church, which owned it. So another Complaint was now launched to the highest authority in the church, the General Assembly, which met once a year, some months later. The church officials, wanting if possible to avoid a theological dispute, managed to get it treated as an administrative rather than a theological issue: was each Presbytery entitled to decide for itself who to admit to its membership? The answer in the end was yes, and the Synod's decision was reversed and the local Presbytery's original decision upheld. So all was well. But for a while the case had been all over the press and I had spent time doing interviews and answering numerous letters of support or condemnation.

DAVID: It must all have been rather scary.

JOHN: Actually, not really. The whole affair seemed to me basically ridiculous, something that might have been understandable in the middle of the nineteenth century but not in the middle of the twentieth. And as soon as I knew that the matter was being heard by the General Assembly's judicial commission, rather than its theological commission, I knew what the outcome would be. And even if we had lost I was reasonably confident of being able to move to another suitable job. In fact, I had already been offered one at a university in Texas, and others would come over the horizon if the occasion arose.

DAVID: Anyway, that was the end of your troubles.

JOHN: Not quite. Many years later I returned from Britain to teach at the Claremont Graduate University near Los Angeles. The question again arose of applying to join the local Presbytery of San Gabriel. Not wanting to waste time in futile controversy I consulted colleagues who were members of the presbytery, and they all assured me that the thing would go through on the nod without discussion. But, as it turned out, they were wrong. The local fundamentalists remembered my 'Affair with the Virgin' of more than twenty years earlier and mounted a protest after I had been accepted into the Presbytery. The main issue this time was not the virgin birth but my attitude to other religions. The Jewish community in LA was the third largest in the world, after Tel Aviv and New York, and I had organized a Jewish-Christian-Muslim dialogue group in the Los Angeles area. There was also quite a large Buddhist community with whom I was developing a relationship. I held that Christianity was not the only path to salvation. This was completely unacceptable to the more conservative brethren. In the end the relevant committee asked me if I would withdraw my application in the interests of Church unity, and I agreed to do so. I didn't want to spend my time and energy on an ecclesiastical quarrel – and was also quite happy not to have to attend Presbytery meetings! So I left them to it, and got on with my teaching and writing. But all this was small beer compared with the experience of some of my liberal friends in other churches.

DAVID: Such as? I find the way in which you Christians can hate one another quite fascinating.

JOHN: I know. It's shocking. But, for example, a German Catholic friend of mine was teaching in the Catholic faculty of theology at Munich University. He wrote his thesis for a second doctorate – Dr Habil – which entitles its holder to apply for a professorship, and in his thesis he analysed and defended religious pluralism. Before the public examination by his colleagues the Archbishop of Munich rang up the head of the faculty to tell him not to pass the thesis because it was contrary to the teachings of the church. However, they did pass him. The Archbishop then refused to give my friend the certificate needed to apply for a professorship in a Catholic faculty. He couldn't apply to a Protestant faculty – they were then all either one or the other – because he was a Catholic. And he couldn't stay where he was because the job had a time limit. So it looked as though his academic career was at an end. And it very probably would have been if a new chair had not been created in a British university, to which he was appointed.

DAVID: He was lucky. But what a light it throws on the Church!

JOHN: Indeed. And another Catholic friend has had to retire early from a Catholic university in America because of continuous pressure from the Vatican to sack him because he also advocates religious pluralism. Both the university and the local bishop resisted the pressure as long as they could. But, as I say, it ended with his retiring early. But he too has gone to a chair in a non-Catholic institution. And then there is the case of the enormously learned Jesuit professor Roger Haight who wrote an excellent book called

Jesus Symbol of God, again including an acceptance of religious pluralism, and he is now under investigation by the Vatican. He too has had to move to a non-Catholic institution. There is also the most famous case of all, Hans Küng, the horrific details of which he has recently written in the second volume of his Memoirs.[3] And there have been quite a number of others.

DAVID: Well, that's Christianity today, particularly Roman Catholic Christianity. But I've already reminded you, referring to both Protestant and Catholic branches of Christianity, about the persecutions of the Jews, the burning of heretics, the suppression of women, the crusades, the support for every war and so on.

JOHN: Yes, this is all true. But at the same time if you were to go into a local Catholic parish in any country, where theology is not an issue for ordinary lay people, you would probably find sacrificial service going on by many priests. And likewise with any Anglican parish.

DAVID: That may be. But now let's look at the other religions, particularly Islam, which we were talking about last time. You were telling me about a Muslim reformer, but what about Islam as a whole? Wasn't this spread by the sword in its early days, millions forced to convert?

JOHN: No, that's often said, but it is not the actual history. Let me quote to you from the authoritative *Encyclopedia of Religion*:

> [After Muhammad's death,] [t]he tribesmen's energies were turned outwards in conquest of neighboring lands

under the banner of Islam, which provided the necessary zeal for rapid military and political expansion. Within a century of the Prophet's death, Muslim Arabs were administering an empire stretching from the southern borders of France through North Africa and the Middle East, across Central Asia and into Sind. Muslim rule in the conquered territories was generally tolerant and humane; there was no policy of converting non-Muslims to Islam. The purpose of *jihad* was not conversion but the establishment of Muslim rule. Nonetheless, partly because of certain disabilities imposed by Islamic law on non-Muslim subjects (mainly the *jizah*, or poll-tax – although they were exempt from the *zakat*, or alms levied on Muslims, the *jizah* was the heavier of the two, particularly on the lower strata of the population) and partly because of Islamic egalitarianism, Islam spread quickly after an initial period during which conversions were even sometimes discouraged. This was the first phase of the spread of Islam.[4]

DAVID: Okay. But it is true, isn't it, that under sharia law women are treated much less favourably than men, and that there are barbarous punishments like flogging, chopping off a thief's hand and stoning to death a woman taken in adultery?

JOHN: Yes, and in the most conservative Muslim country, Saudi Arabia, all this still exists. In others, such as Iran, it is still on the statute books, but hardly ever practised – though there have fairly recently been some hangings of homosexuals there. Or were they, as some say, paedophiles? In others again, such as Indonesia, such things are unknown, sharia being observed only in the one province of Aceh. In Indonesia the comparatively small non-Muslim minorities are treated with respect, and the numerous national holidays include Christmas Day, Good Friday and Ascension Day. This tolerant spirit may well be due to the Sufi influence, which originally brought Islam to Indonesia. Other Muslim countries fall between these two extremes.

DAVID: So the scene is rather more varied than I realized. But it includes some pretty awful horrors.

JOHN: It does, particularly in Saudi Arabia since the 1980s. Not only are the traditional sharia punishments used, but the position of women is deplorable – they can't drive cars, can't travel abroad without a male guardian and so on. But in the rest of the Muslim world there is a growing reform movement, based on new ways of understanding the Qur'an. It is increasingly recognized in reform-minded circles that many of the revelations that came to the Prophet Muhammad came in particular historical situations to solve practical problems facing him in his leadership of the new Muslim community in Medina and later on his return to Mecca. They refer to specific situations, and it is a mistake to see them as prescriptions for all situations throughout all time, according to Dr Souroush's teaching, as we saw last time. This is a very liberating thought for Muslims. It means, among other things, that the Qur'anic prescriptions about punishments, the place of women and so on can be superseded in the very different historical and social circumstances of today. Again, several Muslim thinkers, such as Mahmut Aydin,[5] distinguish between *islam*, which is the universal principle of recognizing, revering and obeying God, and *Islam* as the institutionalized religion founded by the Prophet

Muhammad. What remains permanently valid is the basic religious teaching of the unity and absolute sovereignty of God, who is, as every surah (except one) of the Qur'an says in its opening verse, *rahman, rahim,* gracious and merciful.

DAVID: But presumably the reform movement does not affect the great majority of Muslims, who still live in relatively poverty-stricken traditional societies, with comparatively little education – and no contact with the reformers?

JOHN: Yes, that's right. Most of the world's billion plus Muslims are poor, many are refugees, many ill educated and are taught by highly traditional imams.

DAVID: And how is it that in Iraq we have Muslims killing Muslims, Sunnis fighting against Shias?

JOHN: Well, how was it that until recently we had Christians killing Christians in Northern Ireland, Catholics fighting against Protestants? It was political rather than religious, was it not, with the religious identities serving as banners under which to fight for power? Same in Iraq. The Sunni minority were fighting against a takeover of power by the Shia majority.

DAVID: Okay. But now what about Muslim terrorism? The suicide bombers?

JOHN: Yes, a dreadful and disturbing phenomenon. In Iraq and Afghanistan it's a method of warfare, made possible by a powerful religious, or more broadly ideological, motivation. I say ideological because previous suicide bombers – the Japanese kamakazi pilots who crashed their planes loaded with explosive into US warships, and the Tamil Tigers in Sri Lanka – seem to have been motivated more by political than purely religious influences. And of course in all the European wars, right up to the Second World War within living memory, we had Christians fighting against Christians, for political rather than religious reasons.

DAVID: But can you understand the psychology of the young Muslim men – and also women – who deliberately sacrifice their lives to kill others who they see as enemies of their people?

JOHN: Barely. I think I can perhaps understand it intellectually, but not emotionally. They feel that Islam is under attack by the West. They see Western armies invading Muslim countries – Iraq and Afghanistan. They see the West, in the form of the United States, consistently supporting Israel in its illegal occupation of Palestinian territory, still developing illegal settlements, besieging and undermining the economy of Gaza, and so on.

DAVID: Why do you, or they, say 'illegal'?

JOHN: Because in 1949 the United Nations established internationally recognized borders, with the 'green line' dividing Israeli from Palestinian land. This gives the West Bank, Gaza and east Jerusalem to Palestine. It's because Israel has illegally taken over east Jerusalem that there are no Western embassies in Jerusalem – they're all in Tel Aviv. I used to visit Israel, though I don't want to go there again so long as the present Israeli government, or any like it, is in power.

DAVID: Well, we could go on for ever discussing the Israeli-Palestinian problem. I think it's clear that the only possible long-term solution is two states living side by side, with both able to flourish economically. And peace there must be the key to peace in the whole Middle East.

JOHN: Yes, I agree. So moving on now, in the case of Judaism there was the early period, recorded in the Torah, of brutal conquest, followed much later by the diaspora when the Jews have been spread around Europe, Russia and North America, and finally the foundation of the state of Israel, which we've been talking about.

When we look to the East, the different strands of religion in India which are comprehensively called Hinduism have been mutually tolerant, but are all disfigured by the caste system, and have been involved in violence in response to the Muslim invasion of India in the thirteenth to sixteenth centuries CE. But Indian religion has produced inspiring saints, such as Kabir and Ramakrishna and many more, and great thinkers such as Shankara and Ramanujah and again many more. But probably the religious movement that has done least harm in the world is Buddhism, another product originally of India. Buddhist countries have also sometimes been involved in war. But nevertheless the overall influence of Buddhism has been good. The Buddhist emperor Ashoka, about two centuries after the death of the Buddha, decreed that he

> does not value gifts and honors as much as he values this – that there should be growth in the essentials of all religions ... Whoever praises his own religion, due to excessive devotion, and condemns others with the thought 'Let me glorify my own religion', only harms

his own religion. Therefore contact (between religions) is good. [He] desires that all should be well-versed in the good doctrines of other religions.[6]

Chinese religion in its various forms has also been largely peaceful.

But the broad pictures is that the religions, as historical entities, all have their times of flourishing and their times of decline, so that at any given moment some are more flourishing than others.

DAVID: It's a bewilderingly mixed scene. Maybe, as you say, the historical religions have done about equal amounts of good and harm to the human race. But whatever the balance may be, the whole thing is completely discredited to my mind by the sheer amount of misery and pain and suffering in the world. How can this be possible in a universe ruled by a loving God, or a universe whose ultimate nature is good, as your examples of religious experience claim?

13
Suffering and Wickedness

DAVID: As I was saying, I find it impossible to believe in a loving God, or a benign universe, when there is so much appalling suffering and pain in the world.

JOHN: A huge problem, I agree. Do you mind if we simplify it for the moment by seeing it as a challenge specifically to belief in God, even though there are other religions, such as Buddhism, which are not based on belief in a God?

DAVID: That's okay with me, because the contradiction I want to press is between belief in an all-powerful and loving God on the one hand and the reality of pain and suffering and human wickedness on the other. If God is all-powerful he must be able to save us from suffering, and if he is all-loving he must want to do so. But he doesn't. So he is either not all-powerful or not all-loving. In other words, there is no all-powerful and all-loving being. Or, as someone has written, God's only excuse is that he does not exist! This seems to me perfectly clear.

JOHN: Putting it like that, it does seem clear. But not when we begin to take account of another factor, our human free will. To be a person includes having an essential freedom to choose between different courses of action. It involves being able to choose in a given situation between right and wrong, good and evil. I grant that our freedom is very limited – by heredity, upbringing, all the given circumstances of our lives. But even so, our freedom to choose is still real and essential, and without it we would not be self-determined persons, but simply lumps of animate matter completely enmeshed in the causal continuity of nature. Does that sound right to you?

DAVID: Yes, I suppose so. But what then?

JOHN: Well, if God is going to create finite self-conscious beings, what would be the point of making them as automatons devoid of free will? Surely the only beings worth creating would be beings who can freely respond to his love and be, in a metaphorical sense, his – or her – children? Doesn't that mean that they must be genuinely free to respond to God or not, and genuinely free to respond to one another in both good and bad ways? But the other side of this is the stronger being able to exploit the weaker and create the huge disparities of wealth that we see, so that the world now contains both millions of desperately poor people, and also a fortunate minority, including most of us in the industrialized world, who are relatively prosperous and sometimes very prosperous. It means that all of us are free to be kind and caring or unkind and uncaring in our personal relationships, free as communities to live at peace or to murder and pillage and torture and make war against one another, with all the misery that brings with it. We have the fateful freedom to create or to destroy.

DAVID: But if, for the sake of argument, I grant that, it still wouldn't account for all the pain and suffering that is not humanly caused – diseases, accidents, earthquakes, droughts, floods, cyclones, tsunamis and so on.

JOHN: No, it doesn't, I agree. Though notice that a great deal of this is in fact caused indirectly by human action and inaction. A great deal of disease is due to unhealthy lifestyles; almost all car accidents are due to people driving carelessly or too fast; if people choose to live in earthquake areas – as incidentally I did for ten years in California – they have to expect earthquakes; and so on.

DAVID: Oh, and did you experience any earthquakes?

JOHN: Yes, a few. At Claremont, outside Los Angeles, we were at the tail end of the San Andreus fault, and the major earthquakes were further north. But on one occasion when I was out in the yard – or garden in English – the trees started swaying and the ground felt unstable. In the ancient world they might have said that an angel or a demon was passing by. My wife was out in the car, and the tyres absorbed the shock, so that she hardly felt it. On another occasion, I was conducting a seminar, with about fifteen students sitting round a long table. There was a shock and they all immediately disappeared under the table, which was the right thing to do, with me, then new to earthquakes, still sitting foolishly on my chair.

DAVID: Interesting. But even granted that a lot of this kind of pain and suffering is caused by ourselves, with our free will, yet by no means all is. Why does there have to be cancer – except perhaps that caused by smoking – diphtheria, malaria, hereditary diseases, ocean floor earthquakes causing tsunamis? I feel like old Omar Khayyám:

> Ah Love! could thou and I with Fate conspire
> To grasp this sorry Scheme of Things entire,
> Would we not shatter it to bits – and then
> Re-mould it nearer to the Heart's Desire![1]

JOHN: In response to that let me paint the wider picture suggested by one strand of Christian thinking, the strand that seems to me to make most sense. It has a very respectable ancestry because it goes back to a Christian theologian at the end of the second century, St Irenaeus, one of the early Greek as distinguished from the later Latin thinkers of the Church. Irenaeus suggested that instead of humans having been created, as the Adam and Eve story says, as morally innocent and good beings who then disobeyed God and were expelled from the Garden of Eden, we were created – as we now know, through millions of years of biological evolution – as morally immature beings who were only at the beginning of a long process of growth and development, which is still going on in each of us. So the point of the life in which we find ourselves is that we have the opportunity to grow into better human beings.

DAVID: Okay, but accepting that, again for the sake of argument, it still doesn't explain all the natural disasters, from volcanic eruptions to tsunamis, that are an inextricable part of this world.

JOHN: Actually it does, when we consider its implications. If the point of this life is to be an environment for person-making, what kind of world does that need? Not an earthly paradise where nothing can go wrong, no one can get hurt, there are no dangers, no challenges, no problems. Because it's by overcoming problems and facing dangers, and the pain and suffering they can cause, that we have the possibility to grow as persons. The kind of world that can be the scene of person-making has to be the kind of world we find ourselves in. I don't mean that the world has to be exactly as it is, because it's full of contingencies, but it does have to have the basic features that this world has.

DAVID: Well, one basic feature, and perhaps the most fundamental when we're talking about belief in God, is that God never shows himself – or herself. He never tells us that he's there – he keeps shtum and leaves us guessing. That's not very loving. What would you think of a father who never communicated with his children, never sent them a letter, never even indicated that he was alive? – But I suppose you're going to say that he *has* sent a letter, the Bible, with its answer in the Genesis myth? But do you remember Sidney Carter's lyric?

> You can blame it onto Adam,
> You can blame it onto Eve,
> You can blame it on the apple,
> But that I can't believe.
> It was God who made the Devil
> And the Woman and the Man,
> And there wouldn't be an apple
> If it wasn't in the Plan.
>   It's God they ought to crucify
>   Instead of you and me,

> I said to the carpenter
> A-hanging on the tree.[2]

JOHN: I do indeed. Donald Swan, who sang the words that Sydney Carter wrote, was a fellow member of the Friends' Ambulance Unit during the 1939–45 war, and we were at the same 15th training camp at Northfield in Birmingham. But I'm not going to appeal to the biblical solution, which I agree is no solution. What I'm going to say is quite different. In order for this world to be a person-making environment, it has to be one in which God is not evident. God must have created a world – through the immensely long and complex evolution of the universe – which functions according to its own laws and constitutes an autonomous sphere. God has to keep at a distance from it – not a physical distance but a distance in the dimension of knowledge, in philosophical language an epistemic distance. And the laws of this autonomous world, the laws of nature, are not designed for our human comfort. They are impartial, applying equally to all life.

DAVID: But why? Given a loving creator, why not a world that is specially friendly to humankind?

JOHN: Well, in a word, because it is meant to be a person-making world. You can imagine a world in which when someone falls off a cliff they float unhurt to the ground, where a knife wound instantly heals and a bullet fired at you turns into thin air, where no one ever goes hungry because there is always plenty of food, and in short a world in which there is no pain or suffering. Now in such a world you would not be able to injure anyone, so that, if moral wrongdoing consists in injuring others, there would be no wrongdoing, no such thing as a wrong action. But then of course there would also be no such thing as a right action. There would be no moral choices. And such a world would obviously not be a person-making environment. It would be a Garden of Eden minus the serpent.

Nor would it be an environment in which love, in its deepest sense, is possible. There would be sexual attraction, yes; but there would not be the mutual caring, the willingness to make sacrifices for others, the joint facing of life's problems and challenges that is love in its more profound sense. Or that same love sublimated into love for humanity expressed to some form of special service to the poor or the sick or the dying.

DAVID: Okay, accepting, yet again for the sake of argument, that person-making needs a world with difficulties and challenges and even dangers, yet the actual challenges and problems constitute not only a world in which persons can grow but equally a world that crushes and destroys them – not only physically but also psychologically and morally. People can be so ground down by continual illness, poverty, neglect and the cruelty of others that instead of their experience being person-making it is person-destroying. What was person-making about the Nazi Holocaust in which millions of Jews were systematically murdered? Or the murder of millions ordered by Stalin in Russia and by Pol Pot in Cambodia? Or, going further back in history, were the millions sold into slavery being built up as persons – or suppressed and undermined and crushed? Surely the world is as productive of hatred as much as of love, of pointless destruction as much as of person-making?

JOHN: I have to agree with you there. These things are all evils. But I'd ask you to bear in mind two things. The first is this: the idea that I'm suggesting, that a loving God allows evil as the only way of eventually bringing about freely chosen human goodness, does not mean that each particular existing evil is specifically necessary. What is necessary is a world involving natural contingencies and human freedom. Those horrors perpetrated by Hitler, Stalin, Pol Pot, and in lesser ways by innumerable others, have been part of the cost that human freewill has unpredictably involved. It might have happened to take other forms. And whatever form it takes it has been and is being a huge cost.

DAVID: And what's more, that cost is often borne by the wrong people. Bad things happen to good people just as much as to bad people. Disaster strikes indiscriminately. There is no justice in the way life's evils affect us. Illness, accidents, tragedies come to all. It's totally unfair.

JOHN: It is unfair. Life is not fair. But suppose for a moment the opposite, suppose that calamities happened not indiscriminately and therefore unjustly, but justly and therefore not indiscriminately. Suppose that misfortune were proportioned to desert, with sinners always punished and the virtuous always rewarded. Would this be a person-making world? Surely not. In such a world people would act rightly to avoid punishment and receive rewards. The opportunity to do the right thing *because* it is the right thing, and equally to fall into the temptation to benefit yourself at others' expense, would not exist.

DAVID: Yes, I can see a point there, but it only provokes another problem. Isn't it obvious that if the world's evils do in the end serve a person-making purpose, their sheer amount and intensity is much greater than that purpose could possibly require? There is an excess of human pain and suffering far above what a loving person-maker would allow.

JOHN: So it seems, yes. But consider the paradox that if we could see that life's trials and tribulations serve a person-making purpose, they would not serve that purpose! They would no longer be to us real trials that we have to face and overcome, because we would already know that a greater good is going to come out of them. So in other words, in order for the world to be a person-making environment we must not be able to see that this is what it is. A paradox, I admit.

DAVID: I'm not sure that I understand that complicated, and as you say paradoxical, argument. But even if I grant it, but again only for the sake of argument, here is another problem. Why did God – if there is a God – not create beings who were already good, instead of, as you say, beings who could only gradually become good? Gradually! It took over a hundred thousand years for our species to reach the twentieth century, which was the most destructive in human history. Surely any decent creator would have made naturally good creatures who don't have to go through the often appalling creative process of life as we know it?

JOHN: I'm afraid that wouldn't work, not if the aim was to make genuinely good beings. Wholly good beings, created as such, and not subject to temptation – or empowered always successfully to resist it – would have a programmed but not a genuine goodness. Surely a goodness that comes about through the free decisions of free beings is fundamentally different in nature from a goodness that is ready-made by an outside power? And what would be the point, from a creator's point of view, of making programmed puppets?

DAVID: But still you must admit that any person-making process succeeds, at best, only to a very limited extent. No doubt there are saints who are more or less fully made by the end of their lives, but the vast majority of us not.

JOHN: No, not in this life. As the psychologist Eric Fromm has said, 'The tragedy in the life of most of us is that we die before we are fully born.' If this life were all that's available for the person-making process, then I would agree with you. But all the religions teach that this life is only a small part of our total existence; and the way of thinking about this that makes sense to me affirms continued person-making either, according to the Eastern religions, in many lives or, according to strands of the Western religions, in an 'intermediate state' between earth and heaven. But this is a topic that we shall have come to ourselves before we finish. All that I want to say at this stage is that any religious response to the problem of suffering and wickedness has to include a belief in further person-making after this life.

DAVID: Needless to say, I'm a hundred per cent sceptical about any sort of life after death; but yes, by all means let us have a full discussion about it. In fact, why not next time?

14
Life after Death?

DAVID: So it seems that your defence of religion in face of so much pain and suffering depends on further living after death – something that I find it impossible to believe. I am content with this life, and I don't need another.

JOHN: I'm afraid you're thinking there only of yourself. But consider what Terry Eagleton says: 'the hard-nosed realists who claim that there is no need for another world have clearly not been reading the newspapers'.[1] He's suggesting, surely rightly, that we have to think of the whole of humanity and not just of ourselves.

DAVID: Okay, yes, I accept that. But even if we need another world, that doesn't mean there is one. Do you believe in another life on the basis of evidence? For instance, do you accept the supposed evidence of spiritualist mediums?

JOHN: No, I don't. I have in fact looked at this rather carefully. For many years I was a member of the Society for Psychical Research, whose publications, incidentally, debunk false claims as well as reporting new experiments and new data. I have also sampled for myself both trance and materialization mediumship.

DAVID: That's foreign territory to me. What happens in trance mediumship?

JOHN: Typically, the medium, who may be a man or a woman, but let's say it's a woman, closes her eyes and appears to fall asleep. After a while she begins to speak, claiming to be a departed spirit who is using the medium's body to communicate with the living. The speaker professes to be a 'control' who relays messages from other departed spirits. She describes them, often gives their names, and delivers what seem to be appropriate messages from them. And quite often, with a good medium, these messages do seem to be characteristic of a deceased relative whom you knew well.

DAVID: But nevertheless you don't think they're genuine? Why not, if as you say the messages are characteristic of someone who was presumably unknown to the medium?

JOHN: Well, sometimes the medium was asking me questions and fishing for clues on which to base a message, but sometimes I thought that quite possibly the medium was telepathically sensitive and was picking up impressions from me which she, in a kind of auto-hypnotic trance state, genuinely thought were coming from a deceased spirit. But, at the same time, I have to say that some of the other cases I have heard about and some that I have read about in the early Proceedings of the Society for Psychical Research are much more impressive. So I don't totally dismiss the whole thing. I think it may be possible that when we die what the philosopher C. D. Broad called a 'psychic factor' remains, at least for a while, and could be picked up by mediums.

DAVID: I don't know that I want totally to discount that. But I'd like to hear a bit more about what you mean by 'telepathically sensitive'.

JOHN: Well, first of all, I do believe that telepathy, or ESP, extra-sensory perception, is a reality. Here I'm not impressed so much by the statistical evidence produced by such researchers as the late J. B. Rhine of Duke University, although he did find with a few particularly telepathically sensitive subjects results that were significantly above chance expectation, and I don't dismiss that. But I'm more impressed by spontaneous cases of telepathy, too many of which have been recorded to be explained away.

DAVID: What sort of cases are you talking about?

JOHN: Many of the most striking occurred before the days of radio. For example, a man in India, a colonial administrator, suddenly and unexpectedly dies in an accident, and his wife in England is at the same time powerfully aware of this in a sensation that she has never had before, or sometimes in a dream that night. And then weeks later the news of his death arrives in England, and it turns out that this powerful feeling of her's occurred at the time of his death. Or a contemporary case, told to me by the person involved, is that of a barrister whose much older pupil master was in hospital with terminal cancer. My barrister acquaintance visited the old man every day, and one day when he seemed to be near the end he asked the nurses to ring him during the night if the patient was indeed dying, so that he could come to be with him. There was no phone call that night, but he suddenly awoke at two in the morning and momentarily saw his old pupil master standing there in the room. Next day he went to the hospital and was told that at two in the morning the old man had died. They had not rung him then because it happened so suddenly that it was too late for him to come. Evidently, the barrister's awareness of the death as it happened presented itself to his consciousness in the form of an apparition. And there are innumerable other such cases. So I do believe that telepathy occurs.

DAVID: Yes, perhaps. Though of course if it does it in no way supports religious beliefs. And you said that you had also witnessed materializing mediumship, spirits materializing before your eyes?

JOHN: This was with the then-famous Helen Duncan. It was in the 1930s, and I was 14 or 15. Helen Duncan came to the town where we lived, Scarborough, and a séance was held in our house at the invitation of my parents. In the quite large sitting room a corner was curtained off, with a chair inside it and a dim red light hanging from the ceiling outside the curtain. Mrs Duncan, with a male assistant, possibly her husband, arrived – Mrs Duncan smelling, my mother said, of gin – and was taken into another room and searched by two women members of the audience, and dressed in a simple black dress. She then came into the sitting room and sat in the chair behind the now-open curtain. The male assistant closed the curtain, and the lights went out apart from the dim red light. The audience, about twenty people who had all paid a fee which went to Mrs Duncan, sang some familiar hymns. Presently, there were noises from behind the curtain, and then figures began to appear, one at a time, through the curtain, just the head and a long white robe, saying a name – Robert or Emily etc. – in what seemed a male or female voice. About half an hour later, after eight or so had appeared they stopped and there was a groaning noise from behind the curtain. The male assistant got up and opened the curtain and held Mrs Duncan as she staggered out and helped her into another chair. Several members of the audience said that they had recognized their deceased relatives. The spiritualist theory is that the medium produced a mysterious substance called ecto-plasm through her mouth, which built up into the spirit forms.

In 1931 Helen Duncan had been investigated by Harry Price – not to be confused with the philosopher H. H. Price, who was also interested in parapsychol-ogy – and declared to be a fake. But later, in the 1940s during the war and before the Allied invasion of the continent, she held a séance in Portsmouth. She had claimed to see a sailor with HMS *Barham* on his cap. The *Barham* had in fact been sunk but the news kept secret, so that the authorities wanted to keep Mrs Duncan away from the public until after the invasion.

DAVID: Hmm.

JOHN: Yes, Hmm. However, she had been in Portsmouth before as well as on this occasion, and might have picked up this information from a member – or a friend of the member – of the family of one of the drowned sailors, who had presumably been privately notified that their son was 'lost in action'. The Admiralty was alarmed lest she was genuinely clairvoyant and might reveal the impending landings in France, and arranged for her to be prosecuted under the ancient Witchcraft Act of 1735 – since repealed – and she was jailed for nine months.

The prevailing theory about her materializations was that she swallowed cheese cloth or some other thin substance and then regurgitated it as ectoplasm. My own theory, having attended the séance in Scarborough, was that when her male assistant helped her into the chair behind the curtain he managed to throw her the tightly packed cloth, and to take it back as he helped her out into another chair afterwards.

DAVID: I heartily approve of your scepticism. But if you don't base your belief in a life after death on evidence, what do you base it on?

JOHN: It's an inference from my basic religious interpretation of the universe. If there is a loving God, or – as I think – a benign ultimate reality, it seems to me to follow that human beings, with our moral and spiritual nature, are not a mere accident, existing for a brief moment of cosmic time only to be almost instantly extinguished, with the universe going on as though we had never existed, but we must be part of a process of creating something of permanent value. Human existence must be a project, not a dead end.

DAVID: Which means what for you? That after death we live eternally in heaven – or hell?

JOHN: Actually, no. In fact I don't think that the tra-ditional Christian and Muslim idea – the Jews are mostly today a bit vaguer about an after-life – makes much sense. None of us is ready at the end of this life for either an eternal heaven or an eternal hell. This in spite of the fact that conservative Christians and Muslims, of whom there are many millions, seriously believe that. But no, I believe there must be an oppor-tunity for further moral and spiritual growth beyond this life.

DAVID: Meaning what Catholics call purgatory?

JOHN: No, because according to the traditional Catholic doctrine, in purgatory there is no further moral and spiritual growth such as is possible in an environment requiring moral choices. In purgatory we remain as we are except that we are purged of our sins. But what is needed is the possibility of fur-ther growth. Some Protestant theologians speak of an intermediate state. If that idea can be properly devel-oped it will meet the need.

DAVID: So how would you develop it?

JOHN: Well, moral and spiritual growth takes place within the constraints of a limiting time-frame. Faced with an endless existence there would be no pressure to change, but the limits of birth and death provide that pressure. They mean that if you're going to do any-thing you have to get on with it now. It's our mortality that gives our lives meaning and urgency. So it seems to me that the next life must be another similarly finite life, with its own beginning and end. But then one more such life will not be enough for the great major-ity of us. So there must be a series of further lives.

DAVID: In other words, reincarnation – such as Hindus and Buddhists believe. But we're mercifully free from such nonsense here in the West.

JOHN: Remember that what seems to anyone to be nonsense depends on what culture they were born into. To hundreds of millions in the East reincarnation seems obvious. But in any case the idea seems increasingly to appeal to people in the West. A 1990 Poll by CNN showed that about 35 per cent of Americans then believed in reincarnation. A Europe-wide survey has found that about 24 per cent of Europeans profess belief in reincarnation. This varies from country to country, however, and in Britain it is 30 per cent. He summarizes his main conclusions under four heads. Throughout Europe we find an increasing belief in reincarnation. This belief is particularly found among the younger generation. Surprisingly, the belief seems to be slightly more prominent among traditionally Catholic populations than among their Protestant counterparts. In some parts of Europe one in every five persons believes in reincarnation, while in other parts it is one in three. Another survey found that as many members of the Church of England believe in reincarnation as believe in heaven and hell – though this, it seems, is often more a gut feeling than a developed doctrine.

DAVID: Surprising. Anyway, what does it come to when it is a developed doctrine?

JOHN: You have to distinguish between the popular picture of reincarnation, including the popular Hindu and Buddhist conception, and the rather different idea found in some Buddhist philosophy. The popular idea is that the present self lives again, and may be able to remember a previous life, or sometimes more than one. And there are many stories from around the world, particularly in Hindu India and Buddhist Sri Lanka, of children remembering a previous life. There is also the popular idea of being born again as a lower form of animal life. But this latter has very little serious support.

DAVID: Okay. But what about memories of previous lives?

JOHN: Yes, this has been seriously studied. Professor Ian Stevenson of the Department of Psychiatry at the University of Virginia, who died in 2007, reported in a series of books on nearly three thousand cases, mainly in Asian cultures, of professed memories of a previous life. A typical sort of case would be of a child in India or Sri Lanka speaking about another father and mother, and perhaps brothers and sisters, in another village some miles away, and when taken there the child is able to describe how things had looked a few years ago when he or she claimed to have lived there, and to recognize people and places without ever having been there before in this life.

DAVID: And did Stevenson vouch for any of these?

JOHN: He was cautious. His first book is called *Twenty Cases Suggestive of Reincarnation.*[2]

DAVID: I know that you've spent time in India and Sri Lanka. Did you ever come across any of these cases?

JOHN: Not directly. But there was a famous case, Shanti Devi, a young girl in Delhi in the 1930s. When she was four she said, 'This is not my real home.

I have a husband and a son in Mathurai (or Muttra).
I must return to them.' When the local teacher made
enquiries in Mathurai he was told that a woman
called Lugdi Devi had died there a few years earlier giving birth to a son who, with Lugdi's widower,
still lived there. When an investigating committee
took Shanti Devi to Mathurai she was able to lead
them to the correct house, describe its interior as it
had been before a recent refurbishment, and revealed
private information about the family which no one
outside it would have known. Years later, in 1971,
I stayed for a few days at the Aurobindo ashram at
Pondicherry where I met a retired professor of philosophy, H. N. Bannerejee, who had been a member of
the official committee that investigated the Shanti
Devi case. I naturally asked him about it, and when
I pressed him he told me that although he had joined
in signing the official report authenticating the case
he was in fact not sure that it had in fact been a genuine case of reincarnation. He didn't go into details,
and something interrupted our conversation.

And then when I was in Sri Lanka I met the man
who had acted as Ian Stevenson's translator. He
pointed out to me that Stevenson's visit had necessarily been sometime after the case had become known.
The village welcomed it because it made the place
well known and would bring foreigners there, who
would spend money. And so everyone had an interest in promoting the case. It was also evident to me
that a foreign investigator, whether Stevenson or
anyone else, having to rely on a Singalese translator,
would be unaware of any bias that might affect the
way he was translating peoples' answers. So these two

personal experiences have contributed to my general tendency to scepticism. And I'm likewise sceptical about claimed memories of previous lives under hypnosis. Although there are a few moderately impressive cases,[3] in more ordinary cases the person was so often a famous historical figure – Julius Caesar, Napoleon, Cleopatra, people like that – which is suspicious, to say the least.

DAVID: I certainly share your scepticism. Let's assume that supposed memories of previous lives don't provide any good reason to believe in reincarnation. So why believe in it at all?

JOHN: Well, you'll remember that I distinguished between on the one hand the popular idea, which includes at least occasional memories of past lives, and on the other hand the more philosophical Buddhist idea. Buddhism teaches that there is no permanent self that could migrate from life to life. Rather there is a karmic process which continues after the death of the conscious self, and is re-embodied in a new conscious self. This is a new personality, formed by all the factors that go to make us the unique persons that we are – heredity and the various individual circumstances of our lives. But also, underlying all this, the new personality is also formed by the state of the individual karmic process. I would translate this karmic process into my own terms as the basic dispositional structure that has developed over many lives and is still developing in our present lives. This is our most fundamental moral and spiritual outlook, and it is this that is expressed in each new personality.

DAVID: But if this series of new personalities are not linked by memory, in what sense are they reincarnations of the same being?

JOHN: They are linked by being rebirths of the same dispositional structure. This is the continuant from life to life. But according to the Buddhist tradition there is also an unconscious memory, and in the Pali scriptures, in the Buddha's night of enlightenment under a Bodhi tree at Bodh-Gaya, he remembered all his previous lives: 'such a one was I by name, having such and such a clan, such and such a colour, so was I nourished, such and such pleasant and painful experiences were mine, so did the span of life end ... This was the first knowledge attained by me in the first watch of the night.'[4]

DAVID: And do you reckon that this is historical, or legendary?

JOHN: Well, it seems that shortly after the Buddha's death a council of elders was held to bring together all the different memories of his teachings. This would be in the fourth or third centuries BCE. They were probably first written down in the first century BCE, several hundred years after the lifetime of the Buddha. No one knows for sure how much of the material goes back to the Buddha himself, but probably a good deal of it does. But in any case this particular story expresses the Theravada Buddhist belief that there is an unconscious memory of previous lives, and if so the memory might occasionally leak into a child's consciousness, as these reports from India and Sri Lanka and elsewhere claim. I'm not betting anything on those reports, but I do nevertheless think there must be an underlying thread of memory, which may possibly sometimes emerge in consciousness.

DAVID: And where are all these rebirths supposed to be? They can hardly be in this world because its population has exploded in size, once only a million or two, now about six billion. A population of, say, a million, if recycled, would still number a million.

JOHN: True. But although the early Buddhists were not aware of population growth they did in fact believe in many spheres of existence other than this earth. And today, without having to follow them in that, we now know more about the size of the physical universe with its countless millions of galaxies, each containing countless millions of stars. There may well be intelligent life on other planets of other stars in this and other galaxies. And it may be that some, or even all but one, of our many lives are lived as embodied beings in other worlds, each with its own history, culture, languages, but still with moral decisions to be made expressing the same spiritual/moral dispositional structure that now lives in this world.

DAVID: So this may not be our first life?

JOHN: No, and in fact I would think most probably not.

DAVID: Okay. So going back to the assumption that if there is an underlying memory, but we normally have no access to it, what does that mean for the mortality of our present conscious selves? Doesn't it mean that the present conscious me and the present conscious you are going to perish completely at death?

JOHN: Yes, it does. And that's something most of us find hard to face. We have to learn to accept our mortality, and to think of ourselves as like runners in a relay race, each passing the torch onto the next. In this life we are now carrying the torch, we have the sole responsibility for it. By the way we react to life's circumstances, both fortunate and unfortunate, we are affecting the continuing dispositional structure, or karma, both positively and negatively. We can pass it on in a better or a worse state, knowing that a future personality will be a better or a worse person because of us.

DAVID: That's a lot to ask. I'm not sure if I could accept it, if I believed your theory.

JOHN: Yes, it *is* a lot to ask. It's extremely challenging and demanding. It means doing good, not for the sake of any reward or to avoid any penalty, but simply because it is good; and not being concerned about ourselves, but about the creation of goodness.

DAVID: And what does it mean for people like me, who don't believe a word of it?

JOHN: If it's a fact it doesn't make any difference whether anyone believes or doesn't believe it. It's how they actually live that's important. If this Buddhist scheme is true, we are all the time affecting the karmic process that is currently embodied in our lives, whether we believe that or not.

DAVID: And I, for one, still don't believe it.

15
Cosmic Optimism

DAVID: I suppose it's that belief in some kind of further living after death that is the basis of what you've called the cosmic optimism of the religions.

JOHN: That's certainly an important part of it.

DAVID: But the religions must also be more immediately concerned with our life in this world. How can they speak of optimism when there is so much unfairness, misery and injustice in the world?

JOHN: The answer is that all the great world faiths fully acknowledge this, and yet combine this immediate pessimism with an ultimate optimism.

DAVID: So they are all pessimistic about our present situation?

JOHN: Yes. According to Christian teaching, we are fallen beings living in a fallen world. This doesn't depend of course on a literal understanding of the biblical story of the fall of Adam and Eve. It's usual today – except among the all-too-numerous fundamentalists – to see that as a mythic expression of the observable fact that human nature has shown itself throughout history to be capable of appalling brutality, cruelty and selfishness, so that the world is as we see it today. We've both lived through most of the bloodiest century ever, with hundreds of millions killed in war, and yet millions more dying in famines and floods. Not the worst century because human nature has become worse, but because the technology of destruction is now so appallingly efficient. All this makes it a 'fallen' world for Christianity and also for Judaism. And for Islam the weakness of human nature is evident, for we are frail creatures made out of the dust of the earth, in constant need of the grace and mercy of God. And for Buddhism all life is *dukkha*, unsatisfying, unsatisfactory, lacking: 'Birth is ill, decay is ill, sickness is ill, death is ill. To be conjoined with what one dislikes means suffering. To be disjoined from what one likes means suffering. Not to get what one wants, also means suffering'.[1] And for Hindus we are constantly reborn into this world of so many hardships.

DAVID: Okay, so these religions share the realism of the rest of us in taking a dim view of the state of the world and of our human nature. So where's the cosmic optimism?

JOHN: This is an equally prominent part of the teachings of each of the religions. Christianity has always presented itself as good news – the news that in Jesus God has revealed his love for humanity and calls us to enter his realm. Jesus often spoke about the consequences beyond this life of our actions now. So the idea of life beyond death is also an essential part of Christian teaching.

DAVID: And Judaism?

JOHN: Judaism's optimism has been more for the survival of the Jewish race through their covenant with God and, in the rabbinic Judaism that began at about the same time as Christianity, for an ultimate future resurrection in paradise. A rabbi formulates this 'official' Jewish theology: 'If there is no eschatological unfolding of a Divine drama in which the Jewish people will ultimately triumph, what hope can there be for the Righteous of Israel?'[2]

DAVID: So, roughly, the ancient Judaism of the Old Testament was entirely this worldly, as I've read, but the later and contemporary rabbinic Judaism less so?

JOHN: Roughly, as you say, yes. But Jewish writers today tend to be a bit vague about an afterlife. But so, for that matter, do most Christians today.

DAVID: Okay. And Islam?

JOHN: A Muslim's hope is for eternal life in paradise, a hope resting on the eternal nature of God who, as every surah of the Qur'an (except one) begins by reiterating, is *rahman, rahim*, gracious and merciful. We are morally weak, made out of the dust of the earth, and yet we are created by God, who is 'all-forgiving and all-merciful' (Qur'an 39:53).

DAVID: You mentioned hell in connection with Christianity, and it is equally prominent in Islam. Surely it undermines what you call their cosmic optimism. If vast numbers of people are to suffer eternally, I don't call that cosmic optimism, but at best a highly selective optimism.

JOHN: Yes, I'm afraid you're right. Within Christianity it was for many centuries a seriously held fear, and it still is among many of the fundamentalists – though they never seem to think of themselves personally as in danger of hell! But for the rest of us, an eternal hell has long since ceased to be believed in. It faded out of Christian mainstream thinking well over a century ago. And in Islam the Sufi strand of devotion in particular is open to the thought that hell may be empty. Rumi, for example, tells parables pointing to this – like the story of the man being taken to hell, who turns back at the last moment saying what a terrible sinner he has been but asking for mercy, which he receives and is saved.[3] Always the Muslim clings to the thought of the endless mercy of God.

DAVID: You say that many religious people today are trying to get away from the old belief in hell. But they would be better off never having thought of it in the first place – like we unbelievers.

JOHN: Yes, the idea of eternal hell is indeed a major blemish. I'm afraid that's just a fact. And it also has to be admitted that it goes back to Jesus himself, particularly the Jesus of Matthew's Gospel, though never with the statement that it is eternal.

DAVID: Well, yes, Christianity may, at least since the mid-nineteenth century when, as one historian put it, 'hell was dismissed with costs', be basically optimistic – or, as I would say, a whistling in the dark to keep up their spirits in what is for many, as you've insisted, a tough and hard environment. But at least the Eastern religions are frankly pessimistic.

JOHN: Yes and No. Buddhism teaches, as I said, that all life is *dukkha*, meaning that it is shot through with impermanence, suffering, imperfection, unsatisfactoriness. But at the same time Buddhism is supremely optimistic. Within Mahayana Buddhism the ultimate reality is known as the Dharmakaya, which is the universal Buddha nature, and we all share that eternal Buddha nature but have yet to discover what we already are. Through many rebirths we can all attain eventually to the supreme good of *nirvana,* which is beyond our present state of ego-concern and thus beyond the conceptual system to which it gives rise. But liberation or enlightenment can begin here and now. As we read in the *Dhammapada,* which is in effect the bible of the other main form of Buddhism, the Theravada, 'Happily do we live without hatred among the hateful ... happily do we live without yearning among those who yearn ... happily the peaceful live, giving up victory and defeat ... there is no bliss higher than Nibbana[4] ... Nibbana, bliss supreme ... Nibbana is the highest bliss ... the taste of the joy of the Dhamma'.[5]

And Hinduism – which is really a Western name for the variety of streams of Indian religion – shares the belief in rebirth. We are caught in a round of reincarnations back into this world of hardship and sorrow. This is an immediate pessimism, the prospect of many returns to this life which is so difficult for so many; but beyond that there is the ultimate optimism of the expectation of, in an ultimate liberation, *moksha,* which is our highest good, union with Brahman, the Ultimate.

So the world religions really are different forms of cosmic optimism. In one way or another they all proclaim, in the words of the Christian mystic Julian of

Norwich, that 'All shall be well, and all shall be well, and all manner of thing shall be well.'[6]

DAVID: Perhaps the religions are basically optimistic – you know more about them than I. But obviously this doesn't prove that the religions are true and their optimism justified, does it?

JOHN: No, of course it doesn't. The conclusion of our discussions seems to be that there is no conclusion. I base my faith on religious experience, including my own, while you have never had such an experience and no basis for such a faith.

DAVID: Yes, that's about it. Do you think I'm any the worse for that?

JOHN: In the long run, No; but in the short run, Yes, because you're missing out on the difference that a background sense of the ultimate goodness of the universe makes. Let me give you an illustration of the difference this makes. It's an illustration that I've used before and rather like. Imagine that I go by mistake into a hall full of people and realize to my horror that they are revolutionaries plotting to overthrow the constitution and set up a dictatorship. Most of them are armed with kalashnikovs, and are obviously a dangerous group. This is the meaning of the situation, and my reaction is to feel scared and to keep quiet, hoping that they will take me for one of themselves. But then I notice a balcony above us with silently running cameras, and I realize that I have walked onto the set of a film. This changes the situation's meaning for me. I am no longer frightened, but rather intrigued. The meeting goes on as before and I behave in the same way, but I feel completely differently about it, because it's meaning for me is now completely different. This isn't a complete analogy for the meaning of life, because in my story I notice a new factor, the cameras, which changes the situation, whereas in life we are discerning the meaning of this ambiguous universe as a whole. This comes from our awareness in religious experience of the Transcendent. And this change in the meaning of life does make a huge background difference. It's this that you are missing out on.

DAVID: But of course I see that sense as a delusion. And yet none of us can be completely certain. I retain a degree of agnosticism. I feel like old Omar Khayyám:

> Into this Universe, and why not knowing,
> Or whence, like Water willy-nilly flowing!
> And out of it, as Wind along the Waste,
> I know not whither, willy-nilly blowing.[7]

But don't you also share some degree of agnosticism?

JOHN: I'm conscious, like any rational person, that I may possibly be mistaken, deluded. But my own religious experience, which I told you about earlier, backed up by the experience-based teachings of so many much greater figures, makes me as nearly certain as it is possible to be of the ultimate goodness of the totality of which we are part.

DAVID: Well, I hope you are right, though I still think you are wrong.

JOHN: So it seems that in the end we have simply to agree to differ. Though I think I do now have a clearer sense of where our fundamental difference is. It's not intellectual but experiential. We base our beliefs, or disbeliefs, on the data we have, but we have different data, because mine include my own and others' religious experience, and yours not. Right?

DAVID: I suppose so. But without having any such experience myself, I can't really say. Perhaps one day I may ... who knows? And if I do, shall I be as impressed by it as you have been by yours? Again, who knows?

Notes

1. Defining the issue: naturalism vs religion

1. Thomas S. Kuhn, *The Structure of Scientific Revolutions*, 2nd edn, Chicago and London: University of Chicago Press, 1996.
2. William James, *The Varieties of Religious Experience* (1902), London: Collins Fount, 1979, p. 374.
3. Thomas Hobbes, *Leviathan* (1651), Part III, chap. 32.
4. *The Essential Rumi*, trans. by Coleman Barks with John Moyne, SanFrancisco: HarperCollins, 1996, p. 71.
5. Emile Durkheim, *The Elementary Forms of the Religious Life* (1912), London: George Allen & Unwin, 1954, p. 206.
6. Karl Marx, *Critique of Hegel's Philosophy of Right* (1843–44), Introduction.
7. Sigmund Freud, *Civilization and Its Discontents*, in *Works*, London: Hogarth Press, 1953, Vol. XXI, p. 72.
8. Ludwig Wittgenstein, *Tractatus Logical-Philosophicus* (1921), trans. C. K. Ogden, New York: Kegan Paul, 6.44, p. 187.

2. Can God's existence be proved?

1. Anselm, in *Proslogion*, chapters 2 and 3, and *Reply* to Gaunilo (*St Anselm's Proslogion*, trans. M. J. Charlesworth, Oxford: Clarendon Press, 1965).
2. John Hick, *Who or What Is God?*, London: SCM Press, 2008, chap. 14.
3. Martin Rees, *Our Cosmic Habitat*, London: Weidenfeld & Nicholson, 2002, pp. 80–2.
4. Rees, *Our Cosmic Habitat*, p. xvii.
5. Richard Swinburne, *The Existence of God*, Oxford: Clarendon Press, 1979.
6. Richard Swinburne, *Is There a God?*, Oxford: Oxford University Press, 1996.

3. What do we mean by God?

1. David Hume, 'Essay on Miracles'.

4. Religion without transcendence?

1. Donwi is a conflation of Don Cupitt and the late Dewi Phillips. Donwi's position is not identical with that of either, but draws upon the published views of both.
2. Don Cupitt, *Taking Leave of God,* London: SCM Press, 1980, p. 9.
3. Ibid., p. 57. Don has since gone far beyond this in subsequent books, but retaining his anti-realist conviction.
4. Ibid., p. 50.
5. Ludwig Feuerbach, *The Essence of Christianity* (1841), trans George Eliot, New York: Harper, 1957, p. 11.
6. Ibid., p. 14.
7. Ibid., pp. 55–6.
8. D. Z. Phillips, *Death and Immortality*, London: Macmillan and New York: St Martin's Press, 1970, p. 49. Dewi has also gone far beyond this in many later books, but without withdrawing from this position.
9. Terry Eagleton, *The Gatekeeper: A Memoir*, London: Allen & Unwin, 2001, p. 14.
10. Bertrand Russell, *Mysticism and Logic*, London: Edward Arnold, 1918, pp. 47–8. Referring to this early essay in a 1962 letter Russell said, 'My own outlook on the cosmos and on human life is substantially unchanged', *Autobiography,* Vol III, London: Allen & Unwin, 1969, pp. 172–3.

5. Religious experience

1. In Britain a 1978 National Opinion Poll of about 2,000 people found that 36 per cent reported such experiences. (For details see David Hay, *Exploring Inner Space*, Harmondsworth: Penguin Books, 1982, chap. 8.) In the United States a 1975 National Opinion Research Center enquiry found that 35 per cent reported experiencing 'a spiritual force', and a Princeton Research Center survey in 1978 likewise reported 35 per cent. In Australia in 1983 Morgan Research, which is the Australian

associate of Gallup International, found 44 per cent (David Hay, *Religious Experience Today*, London: Mowbray, 1990, p. 79).

2. Hay, *Religious Experience Today*, pp. 56–7.

3. Michael Paffard, *The Unattended Moment*, London: SCM Press, 1976; Alister Hardy, *The Spiritual Nature of Man*, Oxford: Clarendon Press, 1979; Hay, *Exploring Inner Space*; Hay, *Religious Experience Today*; David Hay, *Something There: The Biology of the Human Spirit*, London: Darton, Longman & Todd, 2006; Meg Maxwell and Verena Tschudin, eds, *Seeing the Invisible: Modern Religious and Other Transcendent Experiences*, London: Arkana (Penguin Books), 1990; and Occasional Papers published by the Religious Experience Research Centre, Dept. of Theology & Religious Studies, University of Wales, Lampeter, Ceredigion SA48 7ED.

4. Hay, *Religious Experience Today*, pp. 75–6.

5. Maxwell and Tschudin, *Seeing the Invisible*, p. 47.

6. Maxwell and Tschudin, *Seeing the Invisible*, p. 52.

7. Samir Okasha, 'What Makes Good Guys So Nice?, *Research News & Opportunities in Science and Theology*, Vol. 3, No. 5 (January 2003), p. 19.

8. Ibid.

9. Ibid., p. 21.

10. Richard Dawkins, *The God Delusion*, London: Bantam Press, 2006.

11. Hay, *Religious Experience Today*, p. 58.

12. For an example of a vision of Krishna, see Klaus Klostermaier, *Hindu and Christian in Vrindaban*, London: SCM Press, 1969, p. 31.

13. Maxwell and Tschudin, *Seeing the Invisible*, p. 61.

14. *The Autobiography of Teresa of Avila*, trans. Alison Peers, New York: Image Books, 1960, pp. 238–9.

6. Trusting religious experience

1. Richard Dawkins, *The God Delusion*, London: Bantam Press, 2002, p. 50.

2. Keith Ward, *Why There Almost Certainly Is a God*, Oxford: Lion Press, 2008, p. 28.

3. Late seventeenth and early eighteenth century.

4. Bertrand Russell, *Human Knowledge: Its Scope and Limits*, London: Allen & Unwin, 1948, p. 180.

5. David Hume, *A Treatise of Human Nature*, ed. L. A. Selby-Bigge, 2nd edn (Oxford: Clarendon Press, 1896), Book I, section 2, p. 187.

7. Despite the religious contradictions?

1. Ludwig Wittgenstein, *Philosophical Investigations*, trans. Elizabeth Anscombe, Oxford: Blackwell, 1953, p. 194.
2. Andrew Newberg and Eugene d'Aquili, *Why God Won't Go Away: Brain Science and the Biology of Belief,* New York: Ballantine Books, 2001, pp. 2–7.
3. D. T. Suzuki, *Zen Buddhism*, ed. William Barrett, Garden City, NY: Doubleday, 1956, p. 84.
4. Quoted by William James, *The Varieties of Religious Experience* (1902), London: Collins, 1960, p. 248.
5. Ibid., p. 17.
6. Thomas Aquinas, *Summa Theologica*, II/II, Q. 1, art 2.
7. *Songs of Kabir*, trans. Rabindranath Tagore, New York: Samuel Weiser, 1977, p. 75.
8. Meister Eckhart, Sermon 27, *Meister Eckhart: The Essential Sermons*, trans. Edmund Colledge and Bernard McGinn, Mahwah, NJ: Paulist Press, 1981, p. 225.
9. Meister Eckhart, Sermon 1. Raymond Blakney, *Meister Eckhart, a Modern Translation*, New York: Harper & Row, 1941, p. 225.
10. Gershom Scholem, 'General Characteristic of Jewish Mysticism', in Richard Woods, ed., *Understanding Mysticism*, New York: Image Books, 1980, p. 149.
11. Ibn al-'Arabi, *Bezels of Wisdom*, trans. John Farina, London: SPCK, 1980, p. 92.
12. Quoted by Paul Knitter, *Without Buddha I Could Not Be a Christian*, Oxford: One World, 2009, p. 15.
13. Qur'an 2:176–7.
14. *The Middle Length Sayings* (*Majjhima-Nikaya*), trans. I. B. Horner, London: Luzac (Pali Text Society), 1954, p. 46.
15. It was Helda Camera who said, 'When I give food to the poor, they call me a saint. When I ask why the poor have no food, they call me a communist.'

8. Neuroscience and religious experience

1. Ian Cotton, 'Dr Persinger's God Machine', *Independent on Sunday*, 2 July 1995.
2. Rita Carter, *Consciousness*, London: Weidenfeld & Nicholson, 2002, p. 288.

3. V. S. Ramachandran, *Phantoms in the Brain*, New York: William Morrow, 1998, p. 175.
4. Ibid., p. xvii.
5. Roger Penrose, 'Can a Computer Understand?', in Steven Rose, ed., *From Brains to Consciousness*, London: Penguin, 1999, p. 14.
6. Steven Rose, 'Brains, Minds and the World', in Rose, ed., *From Brains to Consciousness*, p. 14.
7. Benjamin Libet, 'Do We Have Freewill?' in Benjamin Libet, Anthony Freeman and Keith Sutherland, *The Volitional Brain*, Thorverton: Imprint Academic, 1999, pp. 55–6.
8. Aphorism 40, in the Vatican Collection.

9. More on neuroscience

1. William James, *The Varieties of Religious Experience* (1902), London: Collins Fount, 1999, p. 373.
2. Ray Jordan, 'LSD and Mystical Experience', in John White, ed., *The Highest State of Consciousness*, New York: Doubleday, 1972, p. 284.
3. Single photon emission computed tomography.
4. Andrew Newberg, Eugene d'Aquili and Vince Rause, *Why God Won't Go Away: Brain Science and the Biology of Belief*, New York: Ballentine Books, 2001, pp. 3–8.
5. James H. Austin, *Zen and the Brain*, Cambridge, Mass: MIT Press, 1998, p. 23.
6. Ibid., p. 35.
7. Ibid., pp. 35–6.
8. John Oman, *The Natural and the Supernatural*, Cambridge: Cambridge University Press, 1931, p. 199.

10. Implications for Christianity

1. Joshua 10:12–14.
2. John 10:30.
3. John 14:9.
4. John 14:6.
5. John 8:58.
6. Mark 10:18.
7. John 10:1–6.
8. Matthew 28:17.
9. Matthew 27:52–3.

10. 1 Corinthians 15:8.
11. Acts 22:6–9.
12. 1 Corinthians 15:6.
13. 1 Corinthians 15:44 and 50. All biblical quotations taken from the Revised Standard Version, 2nd edn (1971).

11. Implications for Islam

1. All my quotations from Soroush are taken from Abdolkarim Soroush, *The Expansion of Prophetic Experience*, translated by Nilou Mobasser, Leiden and Boston: Brill, 2009.
2. Rumi, *Rumi, Poet and Mystic*, trans. R. A. Nicholson, London: Unwin, 1978, p. 166.
3. *Fiqh* = shariah, law.
4. Abdolkarim Soroush, *Reason, Freedom, and Democracy in Islam*, Oxford and New York: Oxford University Press, 2000.

12. The religions: good or bad?

1. Wilfred Cantwell Smith, *The Meaning and End of Religion*, 1962, Minneapolis: Fortress Press, 1991.
2. Blaise Pascal, *Pensées*, trans. F. W. Trotter, London: J. M. Dent, 1932, No. 894, p. 265.
3. Hans Küng, *Disputed Truth* (2007), trans John Bowden, New York: Continuum, 2008.
4. *The Encyclopedia of Religion*, ed. Mircea Eliade, Macmillan: 1987, Vol. 7, p. 305.
5. Mahmoud Aydin, 'Islam and Diverse Faiths: A Muslim View', in Perry Schmidt-Leukel and Lloyd Ridgeon, ed., *Islam and Inter-Faith Relations*, London: SCM Press, 2007.
6. *The Edicts of King Asoka*, trans. S. Dhammika, Kandy: Buddhist Publication Society, 1993, Twelfth Rock Edict.

13. Suffering and wickedness

1. Edward Fitzgerald, *The Rubbáiyát of Omar Khayyám*, 1st edn (1859), 73.
2. Sydney Carter, 'Friday Morning' © Stainer & Bell.

14. Life after death?

1. Terry Eagleton, *The Gatekeeper: A Memoir*, London: Penguin Press, 2001, p. 14.
2. Ian Stevenson, *Twenty Cases Suggestive of Reincarnation*, 1st edn 1966, 2nd edn 1974, New York: American Society for Psychical Research.
3. See, e.g., Sylvia Cranston and Carey Williams, *Reincarnation*, New York: Julian Press, 1984, chap. 7.
4. *Majjhima-Nikaya*, I. 22, trans. I. B. Horner, *The Collection of the Middle Length Sayings*, Vol. 1, London: Luzac & Co., 1954, p. 28.

15. Cosmic optimism

1. Edward Conze's translation of part of the Buddha's first sermon, in Edward Conze, *Buddhism, Its Essence and Development*, New York: Harper Torchbooks, 1975, p. 43.
2. Rabbi Dan Cohn-Sherbok, 'Death and Immortality in the Jewish Tradition', in Paul Badham and Linda Badham, eds, *Death and Immortality in the Religions of the World*, New York: Paragon Press, 1987, p. 34.
3. *Rumi: Poet and Mystic*, trans. R. A. Nicholson, London: Unwin, 1978, pp. 56–7.
4. *Nibbana* is the Pali for what in Sanscrit is *nirvana*.
5. *Dhammapada*, chap. 15, trans. Narada Thera, 2nd edn, Colombo: Vajiranama, 1972.
6. Julian of Norwich, *Showings*, ed. Edmund Colledge, New York: Paulist Press, 1978, p. 225 (Long text, chap. 27), and appearing many times in both Long and Short texts.
7. Edward Fitzgerald, *The Rubáiyát of Omar Khayyám*, 1st edn (1859), verse 29.

Index